SECRETS OF WINNING THE REAL ESTATE NEGOTIATION GAME©

By
SETH G. WEISSMAN
and
NED BLUMENTHAL

Secrets of Winning the Real Estate Negotiation Game

© 2006 by Seth G. Weissman and Ned Blumenthal

Weissman, Nowack, Curry & Wilco, LLC

www.wncwlaw.com

ISBN 0-9765841-1-5

Book and cover design by Miller Communications, Inc.

Printed in Canada

First Printing, Hardcover, May 2006

DEDICATION

This book is dedicated to our spouses, who have always encouraged us to pursue our dreams.

DISCLAIMER

While this book is published by the Georgia Association of REALTORS,® the views expressed herein are solely those of the authors.

ACKNOWLEDGMENT

The authors wish to gratefully acknowledge Cheryl Post, whose assistance in editing this book was invaluable.

ABOUT THE AUTHORS

Seth Weissman and Ned Blumenthal are principals in the real estate law firm of Weissman, Nowack, Curry & Wilco, P.C., located in Atlanta, Georgia. Seth serves as general counsel to the Georgia Association of REALTORS.® He also represents numerous real estate brokerage firms, Boards of REALTORS,® builders and developers and is considered a leading authority on new urbanism. Ned represents developers, brokers, and agents in real estate litigation.

Seth is a 1979 graduate of Duke University Law School. He is a former chair of the Real Property Law Section of the State Bar of Georgia, and a member of the American College of Real Estate Lawyers. Ned is a former real estate salesperson and a 1990 graduate of Emory University School of Law. They are actively involved in negotiating real estate deals for their clients and teaching real estate negotiation seminars.

The authors can be reached by telephone at (404) 926-4500, or by e-mail at seth@wncwlaw.com or nedblumenthal@wncwlaw.com.

TABLE OF CONTENTS

Introduction

NEGOTIATION AS A CONTACT SPORT

This book is about how to become great at negotiating real estate deals. Negotiating is something we love to do. Some people spend their free time thinking about sports, relationships, or where they are going on their next vacation. We spend our time thinking about negotiation strategies. We argue it, swap stories about it, and debate what works and what doesn't work. For us, negotiating a great deal is tantamount to hitting a home run or winning the lottery. And yes, we know we're a little weird. Clients have been telling us for years that we should write a book on real estate negotiations. We finally decided to take them up on the challenge.

What do we mean by "real estate negotiation"? We will use this phrase to refer to the process by which two or more parties communicate with one another to come to some agreement regarding the purchase and sale of real property. Effective real estate negotiators help their clients sell properties at higher prices and buy properties at lower prices than others. Negotiation is therefore a very valuable skill to have.

It may be helpful to think about real estate negotiation as a professional sport much like, say, football. And it is definitely a "contact sport" rather than a "spectator sport." In football much of the hard work takes place before the game is ever played. Each team has to realistically assess its own strengths and weaknesses as well as those of the other team, and try to develop a winning strategy. There is a lot of behind-the-scenes action – the coaching, practicing, and "getting psyched" for the big event. And there's the main attraction, the game itself, followed by the post-game wrap up. In real estate negotiations the pre-game show involves obtaining clients and establishing credibility to negotiate on their behalf. Behind-the-scenes action includes preparing both the client and yourself for the negotiation. The contest, of course, is the negotiation of the deal itself. We even have something of a post-game wrap up regardless of whether or not there is a successful outcome.

This book is loosely organized along the lines of a professional sports competition, and will give you specific tips, tools and strategies for use in real estate negotiations. Of course, a negotiation is extremely fluid. Some principles we discuss in the "pre-game show," for example, will have significant application during the main negotiation and vice versa. You will be involved in negotiations with a prospective client at the beginning of the process, as well as with the other party in the real estate transaction later on. Much of what we say will apply to both. Remember: the techniques and tools we give you are useful at all stages in a real estate negotiation, and you may have to pull them out of your tool belt at a time other than when they are presented in this book. Familiarize yourself with the tools and you will know when to use them.

Once you've learned the basic strategies and tools for negotiation, and spotted some of the more common mistakes negotiators make, we will move on to the second, unseen game that is going on simultaneously during any negotiation. It is the game that is played out in your own head and we will cover that game as well. This inner game can either strengthen or sabotage the outward game. Learn the techniques and tools by all means, but do not go into any negotiation until you've sharpened your inner game!

This book is primarily written for use by real estate agents looking to improve their negotiation skills. However, it will also be useful for anyone interested in real estate negotiations, including other real estate professionals and home buyers and sellers. We will examine what makes real estate negotiations different from other types of negotiations and explain why negotiating for others is so unlike negotiating for yourself. We will describe the pros and cons of various strategies and styles. By the time you finish reading this book you will understand why developing great negotiation skills is essential for real estate agents looking to keep their incomes high and to add value to their clients' transactions.

In writing this book one of the challenges we faced was our own English language and the use of pronouns. Since it is rather unwieldy to always refer to agents or clients generically as "he or she," and to use the phrase "his or her" constantly, we have made the arbitrary choice to use the feminine pronoun throughout the book unless the context dictates otherwise. We hope the reader will understand our desire to offer a more easily readable book by making this choice.

The tips and techniques that follow in this book will make you a better real estate negotiator if you follow them. We hope you enjoy reading this book as much as we have enjoyed writing it.

Seth G. Weissman
Ned Blumenthal
March 1, 2006

PART I

THE PRE-GAME
SHOW

Chapter 1

GAME DAY FORECAST
Cloudy With a Chance of Decreased Commissions

Real estate negotiations are significantly affected by the business climate in which the negotiations take place. In real estate sales the business outlook controls whether it is a buyer's market or a seller's market, influences the negotiating tools and strategies we use, and impacts their effectiveness. Normally we would not be discussing the current business climate in a book about real estate negotiations because, like the weather, it is constantly changing. But just as major climatic changes are increasing the frequency and intensity of hurricanes, similarly major changes are underway in our business environment that are changing the business of real estate brokerage, and which will forever increase the importance of brokers and agents becoming great real estate negotiators. Our analysis of these potentially turbulent conditions is discussed in this chapter.

Our real estate brokerage industry is changing more quickly than at any time in our recent past. Technology is streamlining the once time consuming process of matching buyers with the available properties of sellers. With a click of a mouse buyers can now quickly find countless properties based on any number of search criteria.

Technology companies are beginning to create data bases of available properties that directly connect buyers and sellers without the involvement of a broker as an intermediary. These changes are causing some consumers to question: a) whether they need a broker, and b) whether the efficiencies resulting from these changes are beng sufficiently passed on to consumers in the form of lower commissions.

To some degree these concerns have been heightened by rising home prices which have driven the dollar amount of commissions (in transactions where the commissions are based on the percentage of the sales prices of properties) to record levels. In response to these changes and concerns, some brokerage firms are exploring new models for pricing their services and are re-thinking the nature and value of the services they provide.

Limited service brokerage companies are emerging as a viable alternative to traditional full service brokerage firms. Limited service brokers are unbundling their services allowing consumers to pay for only those which they feel they need. Basic services such as listing property in a multiple listing service are being discounted by these brokers to reflect the time savings being realized through technology. While limited-service brokers control only a small fraction of the real estate sales market, their market share is increasing. As a result, traditional agents are beginning to experience price resistance when they go on listing presentations.

Limited service brokers appeal to cost-conscious sellers who are willing to take over some of the "leg work" generally performed by brokers offering a more traditional full service approach. This book does not presume to judge or favor one business model over the other. Instead, we are merely observers of a trend. Similarly, we are not predicting the demise of the traditional brokerage firm. Not all sellers are anxious to, or comfortable with, assuming so much of a real estate agent's historical function. Many would still prefer to have someone else be responsible for showing the home, advertising it to the public, answering questions about the property, and facing the daunting task of negotiating sale terms (and are more than willing to pay for these comprehensive services).

Our point is that brokerage firms should be thinking hard about how they can remain competitive in a changing business environment. With the market discounting some of the services historically provided by real estate brokers, traditional brokerage firms need to focus more than ever on new services they can provide and how they can create a greater perception of value for the services they are already providing.

Selling the marketing abilities of real estate brokers in a more focused way is an obvious way for brokers to justify their value. How a property is packaged for sale, the improvements which are made to get a property ready for sale (or to achieve the highest sale prices for a property) and the type of quality of marketing materials all play to the traditional strengths and talents of real estate brokers. We strongly believe, however, that in addition to marketing skills, developing strong negotiation skills is the best way for brokers to add value to the real estate sales transactions in which they are involved.

How will this battle of new and old models in the brokerage industry play out? While no one knows the answer to this question, it is probably safe to say that overall comissions will likely decrease over time. Whenever we meet an agent who doubts this prognosis we tell them, by way of analogy, what happened to the fees of real estate lawyers in Georgia over the last several decades for closing residential real estate transactions.

Less than 25 years ago lawyers in Georgia were paid a commission to close residential real estate loans. The commission was 1% of the loan amount. If the buyer was purchasing a house with a $400,000 mortgage the fee was 1% of the loan amount, or $4,000. While this might seem like a lot of money, it appeared small by comparison to the broker's commission, which at that time was typically 7% of the purchase price of the property.

Discounting slowly crept into the world of real estate closing attorneys, many of whom tried to increase their market share by reducing their fees. The 1% commission gave way to a .75% commission and then to .5%. Eventually the fee to close a residential real estate transaction worked its way down to a flat fee of roughly $400 per closing. On a $400,000 mortgage loan closing the fee of the closing attorney, rather than going up over the last 25 years, has actually gone down by a whopping 90%!

When the discounting began, the old guard of closing lawyers loudly proclaimed that the discounters would never succeed. "Consumers want the best lawyers they can find to represent them," they argued, "not the cheapest. They want their lawyers to have gone to the best schools, to work for the most prominent firms, and to give their clients great service." But to consumers "cheap" trumped "quality" and discounting eventually prevailed. The new business model was launched.

New business models have affected numerous other industries as well, including retailing, stock brokerage, and the airline industry. The transition is now under way in the real estate brokerage business. If the trend continues more and more sellers will be using limited-service brokers to list their property for sale. Percentage-based commissions may be limited to the selling agent who finds the buyer for a property. Discounting may also be seen on the selling side as buyer's agents and referral brokers rebate a portion of their commissions to their buyer clients, or simply reduce their fees to induce buyers to use their services. As a result of the Internet, finding properties listed on a multiple listing service - long considered one of the real estate brokerage industry's greatest tools - is now available to any buyer with access to a computer. The availability of limited-service approaches has made it easy, and inexpensive, for sellers to expose their homes to large numbers of prospective buyers. Paying a flat fee to list a home in a multi-list system resonates with many sellers.

The impact of limited service brokerages is real. They offer a product many consumers want and are selling it for a low fee. The challenge facing traditional real estate brokers is to articulate a clear rationale for why the services they provide (above and beyond putting the property into a multiple listing service) are worth their cost. If they cannot do this, traditional commissions on real estate listings will likely go the way of the 1% commissions once paid real estate closing lawyers.

In response to this changing climate, some agents will choose to join the brokers using the new limited-service approach. Others will follow the more traditional path of offering full real estate marketing services to their clients but will charge commissions reflecting a lower percentage of the sale price. Still others will try to maintain current commission levels by looking for ways to add greater value to the real estate transactions in which they are involved. Having great negotiating skills will be a valuable tool regardless of the approach followed by the broker. After all, of those buyers who opt for the limited services broker and their "menu" of optional services, many will choose a broker skilled in negotiation and will gladly pay an additional fee for such service.

Why do we believe that focusing on developing strong real estate negotiation skills is a great way for real estate brokers to reinvent themselves and add value to the transactions in which they are involved? Our rationale for this is as follows: in business, people who help their clients make or save more money than others can always justify higher fees. Great real estate negotiators should be able to make more money for their sellers by helping them sell their homes at higher prices. They should similarly be able to help their buyers save more money by helping them buy homes at lower prices. The premise of this book is that developing strong negotiation skills is the best, and possibly the only, way for real estate agents to add enough value to real estate transactions to support percentage-based real estate commissions.

The value of negotiation skills hit home during an exchange with a client who always had one of the authors negotiate his larger business deals for him. After completing a particularly long negotiation I mentioned in passing that I was sorry for the large legal bill I knew the client was going to receive. The client chuckled and asked, "Are you kidding?" When I said "no," he looked me in the eye and said, "Look. You just saved me hundreds of thousands of dollars negotiating this deal on my behalf. I have no problem paying every penny of your bill." His comments stuck with me for a couple of reasons. First, few clients welcome large bills. Second, he was right. My bill for legal services was a fraction of what I had saved him. Good negotiation skills had enhanced his financial position. The benefit far outweighed the cost.

This principle has equal application to the real estate brokerage business. In today's competitive environment businesses that survive are the ones that offer greater value to their customers. Of course value can be measured in different ways. The limited-service model gives value by reducing prices and the extent of services offered. Value can also be given by offering more services to the consumer for the same price, or focusing on elements of service that offer a more tangible financial benefit to the consumer. Real estate agents skilled in negotiation techniques bring added financial value to the transaction for their clients. The agent's services are well worth their cost if, through the use of negotiation skills, she can save a buyer or seller tens of thousands of dollars.

In order to survive in the current real estate climate, traditional real estate agents must reposition themselves as professionals with (a) sophisticated knowledge of real estate markets, and (b) advanced negotiation skills, both of which give them the ability to significantly improve the financial return realized by consumers in buying or selling real estate.

Let's look at a different industry to better understand this point. In the investment world, discount stock brokers are thriving by serving a market of do-it-yourself-ers. At the same time many former stock brokers have re-invented themselves as financial planners. More investors than ever are paying large fees to financial planners because of the expectation that they can help clients earn more than their services cost. Both models are succeeding. The difference between financial planners and traditional real estate brokers is that the planners have done a better job marketing the depth of their expertise and the financial rewards made possible by the breadth of their knowledge. They have convinced the public that the added value they are offering is worth the cost.

The real estate agent's message must be that just as a financial planner is valuable for advising consumers on how to achieve their financial goals, the new breed of real estate broker is equally valuable in negotiating the acquisition or disposal of the asset that is normally the biggest component of the plan. Knowledge of real estate markets is no less an area of expertise than is knowledge of financial markets. The ability to negotiate for a buyer or seller is just as important a skill as being able to research the right stock or bond to buy or sell, or knowing how to set up a college savings or retirement account. It all directly translates into financial gains for the consumer.

Unfortunately, the residential real estate brokerage industry has to overcome an image problem. While residential real estate agents

7

are more sophisticated than ever, some buyers perceive them as merely house finders. Similarly, some sellers see brokers as amateur image consultants who prepare sales fliers or brochures and make suggestions about how to dress up a home for sale. These notions may have developed in simpler times when it was often perceived that real estate agents were housewives looking to earn extra money in their so-called spare time. Although a modern real estate brokerage office bears no resemblance to this outdated stereotype, the perception still lingers. Residential real estate agents must work strategically to overcome old stereotypes and to enhance their credibility. They must strive to become (or at least be perceived) more like their colleagues in commercial real estate brokerage who have done a better job of marketing their expertise.

The success of these efforts may turn on whether real estate brokers can convince consumers that negotiating for a client in the purchase or sale of a home is sufficiently different from other types of negotiations to justify hiring a specialist. This may be easier to do than real estate agents might think. This is because to be a great real estate negotiator one must have a level of product knowledge and market familiarity that most non-real estate professionals simply do not possess. Strong expertise will help even a novice real estate negotiator shine, particularly when compared with a buyer or seller without such knowledge.

For those who find this hard to believe we suggest the following role-playing exercise that we use in our negotiation seminars. Give an insecure real estate negotiator a brown bag containing an unidentified object with an unknown value. Ask her to negotiate to sell the item to a second, more sophisticated and experienced negotiator at the highest possible price. The second negotiator's goal is to buy it at the lowest possible price. Let them struggle through the exercise. Surprisingly, they will almost always come to some agreement on price, but the final sale price almost never relates to the true value of the object. How could it? Neither of them knew the value of the object for which they were negotiating. The lesson they quickly learn is that even the best negotiator is operating blindly without knowing the value of what she is buying or selling. Anyone who has tried to negotiate to buy a car without knowing its true value has usually learned this lesson the hard way. This is why product knowledge is so critical in negotiations, and is one important area of expertise a real estate professional offers.

Real estate negotiators also offer the benefit of not being emotionally involved in the negotiations as are the buyers and sellers who negotiate for themselves. This difference alone will strengthen their client's position in a negotiation. And as real estate negotiations become more complex, an expert negotiator can help the client not be overwhelmed by the many voices of the participants - often multiple parties and agents, appraisers, inspectors, and the ever-present family and friends offering advice. This also represents an added value the real estate professional brings to the table, making it easier to market the agent's skill as unique and worth its cost.

Mastery of effective negotiation techniques gives a real estate agent a unique, special, and marketable skill set. Many books have been written about general business negotiations, but very little has been written about third-party negotiations. This book attempts to fill that void by helping you to develop those skills and profit from them. Our next chapter will examine specifically one of the ways an experienced negotiator can add value to a real estate transaction, and demonstrate to a client the cost effectiveness of using a traditional (rather than a limited-service) agent.

Chapter 2

WHY PLAY THIS GAME?

When Willie Stark, the famous bank robber, was asked why he robbed banks his reply was, "Because that's where the money is." So where is the money for real estate agents? Why should real estate agents become great negotiators? Because there's always a profit in making or in saving money for others. Learn the negotiation skills that help sellers earn more money and help buyers save more money, learn to market those skills well, and you will succeed.

In order to market those skills well, agents need to quantify the value of specialized negotiation skills in financial terms that consumers can grasp. Your first negotiation, in fact, may not be with the other side in a purchase but with your prospective client when you make your listing presentation. (In Chapter 8 we will walk you through a process to help a commission-based broker develop her presentation to a seller who is also considering using a limited-service broker.)

Let's look at the following example to see how a traditional broker who is a good negotiator can save the client more money than a limited-service broker. Let's assume that a seller lists her home for $500,000 with a discount broker for a $500 up-front fee. Another seller lists an identical home and agrees to pay the broker a commission in the range of 6% or $30,000. Why would a seller ever hire a traditional broker when confronted with such a stark contrast in price? The answer lies in reducing – and even reversing – the perception of financial disparity between the traditional and discount business models.

Agents need to clarify to consumers that the flat fee charged to list their property in a multiple listing service is not the only commission the seller will pay. In many discount brokerage models, the selling broker is still paid a traditional brokerage commission (which for this example we will say is 3%). In other words, the difference between the two business models more realistically is 6% (or $30,000) versus 3% plus $500 (or $15,500). While the difference is still significant, the gap is starting to close. This is where the negotiating skill and experience of a brokerage firm and its agents comes into play.

There is a wider range than ever in the price for which a property might be expected to sell. With a $500,000 listing the range of possible sale prices may realistically be from $400,000 to $510,000, or a swing of $110,000. While there are exceptions to every rule, it is not unrealistic to expect that the seller, using a limited-service broker and negotiating on his own, will realize a sale price on the lower end of the range, perhaps $450,000. This is because there is often no agent advising or providing representation to the seller during the negotiation. The low flat-rate fee typically covers only the cost of placing the property on a multiple listing service. While some limited-service brokers offer additional add-on services, there is typically a substantial up-charge for such services that eliminates much of the flat fee savings. Many sellers are comfortable with this approach; many are not.

On the other hand, one would expect that a sophisticated traditional agent with special training as a negotiator will help her seller obtain a price in the middle or higher end of the range, perhaps $485,000. With this difference alone it would have made much more sense for the seller to hire a traditional brokerage firm. Here's why. If the seller pays a 6% commission on a $485,000 sale, the seller nets $455,900 (94% of $485,000 = $455,900). If, on the other hand, the seller pays three percent plus $500 to a discount broker, but the seller can only negotiate a $450,000 sale price, the seller will net $436,000 (97% of $450,000 less $500 = $436,000). So, in this case, instead of spending $14,500 more by hiring the traditional broker, the seller would have netted nearly $20,000 more by using the traditional broker. The financial disparity seen at first glance is not only overcome, it is completely reversed and even magnified in favor of using a traditional broker.

The challenge traditional real estate brokers face seeking to preserve the current commission structure is to formally train agents on how to negotiate so that they can use that expertise in the marketplace to sell their services to buyers and sellers. The real estate profession needs more than the authors of this book and a few others who are offering seminars and classes in negotiation. The message traditional real estate brokers need to get across is that: (1) listing or finding a property in a multi-list service is not enough; buyers and sellers need an agent by their side who has been trained as a negotiator when they acquire or market what is, to most buyers and sellers, their largest financial asset, and (2) such agents can save buyers and sellers far more than they cost.

Few real estate agents today are promoting themselves as having special negotiation skills. This may well be because they don't consider themselves to be good negotiators. REALTOR® organizations have yet to develop special negotiation certifications (such as a "Certified Agent Negotiator" designation) for members who complete special negotiation training. Some real estate agents argue that it is not their job to negotiate for their clients. They see their role simply as a go-between for the buyer and seller. This of course strengthens the argument for offering limited services at reduced fees. If you are an agent who does not enjoy negotiating, and you have no interest in developing or sharpening your skills in that area, the limited-service model may be the better model for you. But if you are intrigued by the thought of becoming an all-star real estate negotiator, and by the idea of reaping the reward of higher commissions as a result, read on.

Finally, as part of our "pre-game show," our next chapter will discuss the emotional aspects of a real estate negotiation, and why it is important to understand them.

Chapter 3

UNDERSTANDING THE GAME

Negotiation is by its very nature about conflict resolution. The most common conflict between buyers and sellers is over their opposing goals regarding the price to be paid for the subject property. They may also disagree regarding the timing of the transaction, the length of an inspection period, the repair of defects, the items which will remain with the property, who will pay the closing costs, and the contingencies, if any, to which the agreement may be subject.

When the authors first studied negotiation in law school the process was described as very rational when it was done well. Students were taught to encourage their clients to articulate their goals, share them with the party with whom they were negotiating, and identify points of agreement and disagreement. Disagreements were then to be resolved by sharing information designed to encourage compromise or persuade the other party of the merits of a particular position.

While this academic approach to negotiation is fine as far as it goes, the authors quickly discovered that it bears little resemblance to the rough and tumble world of real estate negotiations. Few real estate agents we know would use the term "rational" to describe the negotiations in which they participate. Many report that their negotiations are often ugly with the parties becoming emotional and at times even acting like children. There are several possible reasons for this, including stress, the lack of relationship, and the theatrics which often come into play. Let's look at these one at a time.

Stress as a Factor

Without any doubt, one reason negotiations are often not "rational" is that regardless of how calm and easy-going most buyers and sellers may appear to be on the outside, most are under stress when they negotiate to buy or sell a property. An agent starting a negotiation without sensitivity to this pressure is in the unenviable position of not understanding her client. Conversely, when an agent can communicate that she understands what the client is going through she establishes trust with her client and enhances her ability to be effective.

So what are buyers and sellers stressed about? First, buying and selling a person's home is serious financial business. Few people ever negotiate the purchase or sale of an item costing as much money. With every offer and counteroffer monetary sums are traded which represent the cost of a vacation, a car, money for the kids' college, or savings in the bank. Second, most houses are not subject to a precise valuation. Every house is a little different than the next and the price at which a house may sell is normally in a range. Sellers tend to think their homes are worth more than they truly are, and buyers think the opposite. Both worry too much about being "taken" in the transaction. Third, at an emotional level, houses have become much more than just a place to live. They have increasingly become a reflection of who we are, our values, our egos, and our status. As such, moving from one house to another can alter a person's self-image, both positively and negatively. Fourth, the process of moving not only involves a lot of hard work, it also involves major life changes. Buyers and sellers are thinking about new beginnings as well as about what is being left behind. Change is always a stressor and is more difficult for some individuals than for others. Some people are also superstitious about homes in which they live. They have a fear that a person's home, like some charm or talisman, will bring them good or bad luck. Others are concerned with whether their new home has appropriate feng shei, or is in harmony with the positive energy of the universe. Many, if not all, of these considerations weigh on and affect a client's ability to be rational during a real estate negotiation.

Clients are not the only ones affected by stress. Real estate agents often join them, being stressed about doing a good job for their clients or anxious because there is a lot riding on the transaction from a personal financial perspective. Being aware of these stressors can help agents minimize the negative impact they have on any real estate negotiation. (We will be dealing with these issues more when we talk about the "inner game of negotiating.")

Lack of Relationship

Another reason why real estate negotiations are not always rational is that, unlike most other negotiations, the parties (and often their agents) are normally complete strangers to one another. They are not familiar with each other's background, personality, culture or foibles. This lack of familiarity contributes to a lack of trust, which always complicates any negotiation. And most real estate negotiations are generally one-shot deals. Buyers and sellers negotiate without the incentive that exists when the parties have an established relationship with one another and want that relationship to continue after the negotiation has concluded. This lack of a relationship is increasingly used by some real estate investors to push for unrealistic price concessions knowing that the worst that can happen is that they will lose the deal and be forced to find another. Many accept this as simply a part of the game and consider themselves to have done well if only a small percentage of deals actually close.

Theatrics

One final reason why real estate negotiations (or any negotiation, for that matter) may not seem rational is that negotiation is also part theater. Negotiating is one of the few activities where a bit of role-playing and posturing is acceptable, even expected, and where open and honest communication is not always encouraged. So, for example, if a buyer is absolutely head over heels in love with a house, her agent may describe the client to the listing agent as "interested" in the property and "considering" whether or not to make an offer. If a seller is desperate for any offer and is willing to slash her price dramatically, the listing agent may casually mention to the buyer's agent that the seller is "motivated" to sell, implying that she may consider a lower offer.

Why is the game played this way? The answer is money. If the seller knows that the buyer will pay any price for a house, most sellers will make her pay dearly. If the buyer knows that the seller is desperate to sell most buyers will only buy at a deep discount. As buyers and sellers make offers and counteroffers and begin to get down to serious negotiations, it is not uncommon for their agents to still describe their clients as less than fully committed and willing to walk away at a moment's notice if their terms are not met. While some buyers and sellers may genuinely be this skittish regarding a transaction, most are not. It is merely the game of negotiation being played.

The keys to successful role-playing are credibility and consistency. Actors must not step out of character or ever admit to posturing. We've seen sellers get up and walk away from a closing table after a buyer bragged about the great deal he'd gotten on a property. Similarly, we've seen the seller brag to the buyer about how they really would have taken much less for a property only to later be sued by the buyers for failing to disclose defects in the property. People don't like to feel like they've "been had" and will often react unpredictably when they do. For example, if the buyer is feigning only mild interest in a property she should not be sending over contractors to be measuring for new window treatments. Similarly, a seller who has indicated she does not need to sell her property and is somewhat firm on price should not suddenly be reducing the price in large increments or at a fast pace. Consistency is essential to a great negotiator. Otherwise the negotiator will be seen as insincere or a game-player, and will damage her effectiveness in representing her clients.

Of course, just because a party may be posturing a bit or hiding her true level of interest does not mean that she cannot change her position. To remain credible, however, this simply needs to be done gradually and in a manner consistent with the original position taken.

The Lesson

What should an agent learn from all of this? The first lesson is that when people are under stress, they have shorter fuses and tend to wear their emotions more on their sleeves. Being sensitive to what the client is going through can help "defuse" a tense situation, and can make all the difference in establishing rapport with the client, allowing the agent to be a more effective representative. Talking to clients in advance about what to expect in the negotiation process and how they may feel as negotiations heat up helps to establish the expertise of the agent as a person who has been there and understands what the client is going through. It also makes it easier for the agent to bring an overwrought client back to reality by nicely reminding them that the way they are acting is what the agent had warned them about much earlier.

A second lesson is to not allow the pressure to get to you and cause you to act irrationally. One of the most valuable skills of a successful negotiator is to be able to show grace under pressure. While there may be good cause to get angry in many negotiations, there is no room for it. Anger (or any strong emotion) interferes with the ability to think clearly which is essential to being a great negotiator. When you feel strong emotions coming to the surface, try counting to ten. If counting to ten doesn't work, count to twenty. If that doesn't work, adjourn the negotiation and wait a sufficient period of time until you regain control. Conflict rarely gets resolved when people are emotionally overwrought.

With regard to the theatrical aspects of negotiation, we recognize that some people are not good actors and that they dislike negotiation for this reason. While acting skills can help, they are not essential to be an effective negotiator. We recommend that non-actors not try to become something they are not, but instead cast themselves in the role of a gatekeeper of information. Such a gatekeeper controls what information should be released in the negotiation and when. Following this approach, for example, the gatekeeper determines (and advises her client) when it is most advantageous to reveal facts, such as a buyer's serious interest in a property, or that the seller is ready to make a major concession on price.

We've always subscribed to the old saying that the best lie is the truth. This doesn't mean that negotiators are required to play an open hand of poker. The gatekeeper's role does not involve lying, but controlling the release of information. If information is withheld (or its release delayed), the ultimate decision as to when and what to reveal should be for the client to make, not the agent. There is no quicker way for an agent to get fired (and deservedly so) than to misstate the client's intentions in buying or selling property without the knowledge and consent of the client.

One of the tougher ethical issues faced by any negotiator is determining just what is appropriate "gatekeeping" to enhance a party's negotiating position. When does it cross the line and become the inappropriate withholding of information that should be disclosed? When is it just plain lying? For example, is it acceptable for a buyer's agent to falsely express only mild interest in a property to try to get a better deal on the price? We would say yes. Is it ethically appropriate for a seller to tell a buyer that there is another prospective buyer interested in the property when in fact there is not? We would say no. Discussions of ethics always involve some degree of line-drawing and hair-splitting. The bottom line is that every negotiator has to act ethically and in the way they are most comfortable.

In Part II we will go behind-the-scenes and show you what type of preparation needs to be done before the actual negotiation of a deal takes place – how to prepare your client(s) and how to prepare yourself.

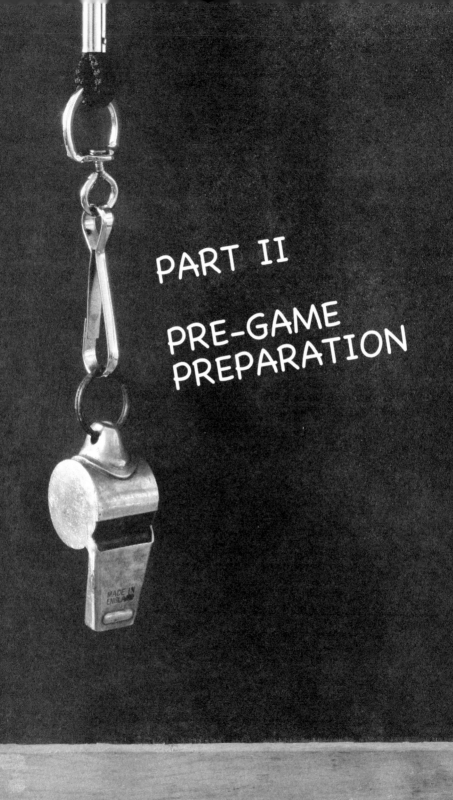

PART II

PRE-GAME
PREPARATION

Chapter 4

THE PLAYING FIELD

Real estate agents' primary roles are to either locate or sell specific properties for their clients. In order to do this effectively, agents need to know the economic health of the housing market generally and of the market or sub-market in which the property is located. This is the context in which their product is being bought and sold. This is the agent's playing field. And familiarity with the playing field engenders confidence – both your own confidence in your abilities, and your client's confidence in you as a professional.

Confidence in your ability as a negotiator is directly related to your ability to communicate your expertise regarding the value of what is being sold. Who would you rather have helping you in a negotiation: (1) a former car salesman who knows plenty about cars and dealerships, but nothing about real estate prices or neighborhoods, or (2) a real estate broker who is very knowledgeable about home prices and trends, but who can't tell a Mercedes from a Pinto? The appropriate answer is "It depends. Am I negotiating for a car or a house?" A car salesman who knows nothing about real estate can not easily out-negotiate a knowledgeable real estate agent, so long as the subject of the negotiation is real estate. If the topic turns to automobiles the car salesman likely has the upper hand. Why? Because of their respective knowledge about the types of products that are the subject of the negotiations.

If you find that you are the least experienced agent in a transaction, focus your energy on becoming the most knowledgeable agent with regard to the property. Your effectiveness as a negotiator will follow.

Your knowledge may start with, but should extend beyond, recent sale prices and community conditions. Develop your familiarity with the neighborhood in which you are operating, by all means, but develop your familiarity with the overall market as well. Agents must be able to intelligently discuss the strengths or weaknesses of the housing market with their clients. When you can demonstrate your knowledge of the wider real estate field, and how that affects the value of a specific property, your credibility as a professional soars. The old stereotypes fade. Your client's trust in you is strengthened – and so is your business.

The type of knowledge that strengthens your client's trust in you is broad and varied. Remember that your knowledge about a particular property always resides within the context of the wider local, regional and national economies affecting the real estate market. Real estate agents must become serious students of current economic realities, and brokerage firms need to do more to train and provide ongoing education on these subjects. Until they do it is up to you as an agent to invest in your own professional future by educating yourself.

There are several steps you can take in this education process. In order to gain a better understanding of your region or city, consider the following:

1) Subscribe to business magazines, particularly those focused on your own geographic area.
2) Join the local Chamber of Commerce and volunteer for a committee such as "new business development" to gain familiarity with upcoming changes in the business climate.
3) Read every report on housing that you can find. Understand the factors considered and the buzz words used by economists and builders to describe the housing market (i.e., the number

of permits issued for new homes, the average length of time homes are on the market before being sold, the average rate of increase (or decrease) in home prices, mortgage interest rates for all different types of loans, the mortgage foreclosure rate, final sale price as a percentage of list price, and the percentage of sellers who pay closing costs).

Similarly, there are several steps you can take to deepen your knowledge about a specific market area within a larger area, such as a particular municipality or a specific neighborhood. Some suggestions:

1) Personally visit every house for sale in the market area in which a buyer is interested.

2) Know the price range of all the neighborhoods in the area, the asking price of each home listed, and whether the asking price is, in your judgment, high or low and by how much.

3) Take the time to personally view the properties listed for sale in the area. You will then be better able to visualize a home's value and communicate it more effectively to clients. After all, buyers and sellers can view the Internet description without needing an agent. No value is added by simply restating information the client can easily find on her own. And of course, no written description in a multi-listing or web site can possibly include everything, or give you a feel for the impression a home makes – positive or negative – when you see it in person.

4) We also recommend that agents study tax and land records to identify recent property sales and tax assessments. Market-specific knowledge is important to the buyers. No one likes negative financial surprises. Helping your clients be informed regarding the full price of a home is adding real value to your services. The better informed the buyers' choice, the more comfortable they are likely to be with their decision and with their agent.

Your clients will appreciate the additional insight you bring them when you have done this homework.

In addition to reading about the economic realities of your area, visiting homes, and becoming more generally aware of market realities, what else can you do to increase your knowledge? Questions are the answer. Get used to asking lots of them. Start with some of the suggestions that follow, then add your own as you think of them. Each geographic region or city will have its own unique factors to consider, but answer the following questions and you will have a good head start on understanding the condition of your particular playing field.

Questions About the Housing Market?

1. Is it a sellers' market or a buyers' market?
2. Is the inventory of unsold resale or new homes going up or down?
3. What is the average length of time a new or resale property is on the market?
4. Is the rate at which new permits are being issued increasing or decreasing?
5. What is the general economic outlook for the area in which the property is located?
6. Are any new large businesses coming to town? Are any existing businesses getting ready to close?
7. Are sales in the particular neighborhood in which the property is located trending up or down in number? In price?
8. What are other agents saying about the strength of the housing market in the neighborhood, city and/or county in which the property is located?

9. What mortgage products are available in the market?
10. Where are mortgage interest rates? Are they heading up or down?
11. Are mortgage credit standards being applied loosely or strictly?
12. Is the foreclosure rate increasing or decreasing?

It is much easier to convince clients you are a good negotiator if you can show them you have expertise in determining the true value of what is being sold. Demonstrate your knowledge of the housing market, explain its value, and clients will put great faith in your skills to represent them.

Now that we've talked about some of the general aspects of the game, let's look at some details of the pre-game warm-ups.

Chapter 5

ALL-STARS UNDERSTAND A PROPERTY'S TRUE WORTH

The best way to help a client negotiate either the purchase or sale of real estate is to know the value of the property. (Remember the exercise about trying to negotiate to buy or sell the unknown object in a paper bag!) Knowing the value of a property means not only understanding the worth of a specific property in its given market but, more importantly, the unique factors that add to or detract from its value.

Some buyers (and real estate agents) assume that a property is worth about the price for which it is listed. This is a big mistake. They assume that if they can purchase the property at a reasonable discount from the listing price they have gotten a pretty good deal (i.e., "I got it for 10% less than the asking price"). From the opposite side, many sellers will set their listing price based upon what their "home sweet home" is worth to them, which may have no significant connection to market realities. Both of these mistakes can be seen in the following example.

The brother-in-law of one of the authors was buying his first home. He found a house he liked and with the help of an agent persuaded the seller to take about 6% less than the listing price of the home. The seller accepted his offer and the deal closed. The buyer thought he had gotten a decent deal for himself. Unfortunately, when he went to sell the property three years later in a housing market of rapidly rising home prices, he realized that the original listing price had been inflated and that he had overpaid for the property. He ended up selling his home for about a $50,000 loss. Neither he nor the real estate agent with whom he was working knew the true value of the property. He made the mistake of negotiating from the listing price instead of the actual value of the property.

In this example the seller's "mistake" of over-rating the value of his home did not hurt him, it helped. But what would have happened if the buyer had engaged a knowledgeable real estate agent who knew the true value of the property? The seller would likely have sold his home for a significantly reduced price (and come away from the transaction feeling very much the loser), or he may have lost the sale entirely if he were not willing to reduce the inflated asking price.

How would a well-trained real estate agent have added value to the transaction?

The obvious answer is that a well-trained real estate agent (for either buyer or seller) would have at least conducted a full comparative market analysis of all home sales and properties listed in the area. She would have researched recent or upcoming changes in the surrounding area to catch any value-enhancing or -detracting events. In the case of the author's brother-in-law, an appraiser managed to initially appraise the property for its artificially high value. Sometimes an agent is a better judge of real estate values in a neighborhood than even an appraiser.

Again, questions are the answer. In addition to thinking about the factors covered in the previous chapter, there are many questions an agent should ask about any particular property she is either listing, or her buyer-client is considering purchasing. The following are questions we suggest.

Questions About Specific Properties

1. Who was the builder? What reputation does the builder have for quality?
2. How old is the property? How many bedrooms and bathrooms?
3. Is the kitchen current in its design and usability? Are mechanical systems and appliances in the home up to date? If the house has outdated features, how easily can they be corrected and at what cost?
4. What is the quality of the finishes on the home or property? Has the property been renovated? If so, when and by whom? If not, what is its renovation potential?
5. Does the home or property have any defects? How costly would they be to repair?
6. Does the home have a garage, onsite parking or offsite parking? For how many vehicles? How does the parking compare to other similar properties?
7. Does the house have good flow for entertaining? Does the house afford privacy to company?
8. Is the house energy efficient?
9. Does the home have a particular charm or character? Are there any unique or special features (i.e., special view, on or near water or a golf course, etc.)?
10. Can the lot accommodate a child's play set or swimming pool? Are there areas for children to play safely?
11. How does the home compare to others in the area in terms of architectural style, room sizes, ceiling heights, quality and maturity of landscaping? How do these items compare with today's styles and trends?
12. How large is the home as compared to others in the neighborhood? How old is the home as compared to others in the neighborhood?

13. How large is the lot as compared to others in the area? Is the lot level as compared to others?

14. Does the lot afford some degree of outdoor privacy to the owner as compared to others?

15. How do the public schools serving the property compare with the public schools serving other nearby properties? How does traffic on the street compare to traffic on nearby streets?

16. How does the crime rate in the immediate neighborhood compare to other neighborhoods?

17. What is the historic reputation of the area in which the home is located as a good place to live?

18. Are there positive neighborhood facilities and services near by (such as parks, hospitals, shopping, etc.)? Are there any adverse neighborhood conditions nearby which would affect the value of the property?

19. Are there any neighborhood or regional changes coming (e.g., airports, new roads, new shopping areas or other developments) which will affect the value of the property?

20. How convenient is the property to regional work, shopping and recreational centers? To major thoroughfares?

21. What are the property taxes?

22. Is the property part of a voluntary or mandatory homeowners' or condominium association? If so, what are the amenities and fees?

23. How does the value of the property compare to the value of other properties in the neighborhood (i.e., is it the most or least expensive home)?

24. Are values in the immediate neighborhood trending up or down?

25. How many other properties in the neighborhood are for sale? If there is an abundance, why?

26. What is the foreclosure rate in the neighborhood?

27. What percentage of homes in the neighborhood sold at or near the listing price?
28. Are there a large or small number of logical buyers for the property?
29. How long has the property been on the market? If the property hasn't sold, why not? Is it price, condition, other factors?
30. What can you ascertain about the owner? Is there any reason to think that this is a distress sale? Has there recently been a death in the family? A new addition to the family? Any signs of a divorce?

One challenge here is that many of these questions seek primarily subjective answers. Buyers also have different priorities and will thus give greater weight to some factors than to others. Nonetheless, these are things an agent should know and be prepared to discuss with her clients. It is amazing how many experienced agents do not know the answers to these questions for homes in the neighborhoods in which they regularly work.

If you are new to the real estate business, try the following exercise in the neighborhood in which you are interested in listing or selling.

Visit all of the listed properties in the neighborhood, answering for each one all of the above questions. Then for each property write down the price range in which you believe the property will sell, what you believe its likely final sale price will be, and how long you expect it will be on the market. Modify your predictions when any adjustments are made in the listing price. Then compare your predictions with what happens in the marketplace. If you regularly engage in this activity, you will become better at discerning the true value of a property in that given area. And if you keep the information you will be creating a personal database that will have real value to both your buyer and seller clients. Armed with all this knowledge you are on your way to being prepared for the next task: preparing your client for the process. We'll look at this in our next chapter.

Chapter 6

PREPARING YOUR CLIENT FOR GAME DAY

Do clients really need preparation? You bet! It is a common mistake to assume that your client understands the way negotiations work in the context of a real estate transaction. While some people seem to move every two years (the parents of one of the authors have moved 28 times), most will only purchase or sell a few homes over the course of a lifetime. It is therefore very likely that your client will have little or no experience with the process. They may not realize that the outcome of a real estate negotiation is influenced by many factors. These include what we say (and don't say), the frequency and timing of our communication, how we dress, our body language, our ability to listen and observe, our confidence level, and our familiarity with the subject matter of the negotiations. Your role is to make sure your clients understand the nature of negotiations, including the inevitable back and forth offers and the role that emotions can play in negotiations.

As lawyers we frequently engage in mediations and settlement conferences, which can be very similar to real estate negotiations: both parties are trying to attain the best deal they can, both sides are to some extent posturing, the stakes can be high, and in the midst of it all, emotions can get the best of people. We find that the best way to prepare a client for mediation is to walk them through the entire process before they get started. The same holds true for negotiating a real estate transaction.

Negotiation Is a Process, Not an Event

Clients (and agents as well) need to understand that negotiation is not an event which occurs only after a buyer decides to purchase a property. It is a process which occurs from the point of first contact between the parties.

One of the authors (we won't say which one!) learned this lesson the hard way when he and his wife bought a house many years ago. Our Mr. X had seen the house in a magazine of nicer homes. He called the listing agent and arranged to see the house the following afternoon. As Mr. X drove over to the property, his mind was going a mile a minute thinking about the beginning of the coming opportunity to negotiate. Mr. X told his wife if she really liked the house he would handle any negotiations. She was more than willing to oblige.

When they arrived at the house they got out of the car and introduced themselves. The house was on a large lot next to a lake. Mrs. X took in the tranquil setting and without even setting foot in the house announced to Mr. X, "Honey, this is the house I want. Let's buy it!" The listing agent hearing this broadly smiled, looking remarkably like the cat that had just swallowed the canary. Needless to say, while Mr. X was able to negotiate some small concessions from the seller, he paid fairly close to the listing price for the property.

Just as the negotiation begins at the earliest point of contact, it also doesn't end when the contract is signed. For some, signing a contract marks just the beginning of getting down to serious negotiations. For a few, the negotiations continue even after a closing or settlement. The lesson of this reality is that it pays to always have a little something in reserve to trade or give up if need be.

How Clients Can Help Their Agent

Since negotiation is a process rather than an event, how can buying or selling clients best help their agent do the best possible job for them throughout the process? Often the best thing they can do is to stay in the background, be observant, and let you do your job. Let's look at how this would play out for sellers, then for buyers.

The best help sellers can be in the early stages of any negotiation process is to let you do your job. Suggest to your clients that they not be present when you show their home. We have seen some sellers, particularly those with sales backgrounds, want to be present for showings to help the listing agent point out the wonderful features of the home or to answer questions about how a particular item or system in the home might work. Just as a lawyer who represents himself has a fool for a client ("honest Abe" Lincoln came up with that observation), the same is true for sellers who hire a broker but then want to do her job for her. When the seller is present for a showing, the message it sends to prospective buyers is: (a) the seller is very anxious about selling her home, and/or (2) the seller lacks confidence in the listing agent to do her job. Neither of these messages increases the likelihood of a successful outcome to the negotiation.

Of course, your buying clients must be present when the house is shown to them, but you can still coach them about what to say (and what not to say) if the listing agent or the owner is present for the showing of a property. Buyers should always be pleasant. As a matter of fact, in many cultures getting to know a person is a critical first step to having any serious discussion about buying or selling a home. People like to know with whom they are dealing. They often first decide whether the person is someone they want to do business with before they ever get down to actually discussing business. It is therefore always helpful for the selling agent and the buyers to be friendly, outgoing, and even talkative about every subject except the property that is the subject matter of the negotiation. (The more they talk or ask questions about the property the greater the likelihood that they may reveal information about their true level of interest in the property or their motivation for buying that could strengthen the seller's hand in the negotiation.)

Buyers should also be coached to avoid making comments regarding their reaction to a home. Many buyers feel obligated to give a running commentary about a property to the sellers or to the listing agent as a way of being polite. Remind them that this is not a social call. Buying a house is an important decision with significant financial consequences. When buyers are overly effusive about a home, start to make comments about how furniture can be placed in a room or which children will occupy particular bedrooms, it is giving the other party far more information than needed and could weaken the buyer's negotiating position.

We also recommend that buyer couples seeing a property for the first time never ask each other "what do you think?" in the presence of the listing agent or the seller. Have them wait until they are safely back in their own agent's car. While many buyers can't help themselves, encourage them to save their questions for later.

What to Expect When Serious Negotiations Begin

In addition to coaching your clients with respect to showing/viewing homes and the comments they should make or avoid, you can also give them helpful information about the ongoing negotiation process itself. There are some general considerations clients need to be aware of as well. For example, they need to know that when negotiations actually begin the process will take longer than they expect. There will be an offer, then perhaps a few days before a response or a counteroffer, then more time before a response, etc. No matter how quickly it may proceed in reality, time often seems to slow down and the other side seems to take too long to respond. The other side will of course be experiencing the same slow-motion effect while waiting for your client's next move. (It's like the old saying: the length of "just a minute" depends upon which side of the bathroom door you're on!)

The client also needs to be aware that emotions are likely to come into play during the process. For example, clients need to know that the initial demand is likely to make them feel outraged, just as their initial offer is likely to make the other side feel insulted. They must remember, however, that the negotiation has to start somewhere and they should not be too concerned with the first number the other side puts on the table.

We all tend to believe that emotions may get the best of others, but not of us. The reality, of course, is that it is difficult for someone to tell when their own emotions are clouding their judgment. Tell clients in advance that you will check in with them throughout the negotiation to be sure they are still on track for the goals they initially set. That way when you see a client acting irrationally, you can say "remember when I told you I would check in to be sure you were making decisions based upon logic instead of emotion? Well, this is one of those times. Let's step back for a minute and see where we are and where we are going."

It's Not About Being Fair, or Even Being Reasonable

Something else clients need to understand is that negotiating is not about being fair, or even being reasonable. It's sometimes completely arbitrary, and that's okay. Your clients need to be prepared for you to suggest some things that may seem to them to be arbitrary limits regarding pricing or timing. Examples of such limits include a buyer telling a seller that, "We've set an upper price limit of $325,000 and simply won't go above that price," or a seller saying, "I will only sell at this price if you can close by December 31st." Of course, whether and the degree to which a party can be arbitrary will depend on that party's relative bargaining power in the negotiation. Knowing that a lack of flexibility is usually not viewed as a positive trait in most business contexts, some parties are uncomfortable in communicating that they have set an arbitrary limit. Some of these buyers are more comfortable telling a seller a little white lie (like they cannot afford to pay more than $325,000 for a property) rather than simply saying that they have set $325,000 as their upper price limit.

The problem with this, of course, is that the listing agent (being trained to be a problem solver), and to a lesser degree the seller, will then try to immediately figure out ways to overcome the obstacle which has been presented to them by the buyers. The seller may offer to take back a long-term, low interest note so that the buyer can afford to pay a higher price for the property. Or the listing agent may try to get the buyers to visit her favorite mortgage lender to see if the buyers might qualify for a higher loan or take advantage of a creative financing program where their mortgage payments would be lower. In other words, the listing agent ends up trying to solve a problem other than the one which is really causing the buyers not to buy the property. When the buyers resist the well-intentioned efforts of the seller and listing agent, these parties often end up rightfully feeling that the buyers are not being honest or not acting in good faith. This can obviously have a detrimental effect on the negotiation.

None of these problems would have arisen had the buyers simply been honest in acknowledging that they were setting an arbitrary limit in the negotiation. There is nothing wrong in the buyers honestly admitting that they like a bargain and would never buy a property unless it was a great deal.

Being arbitrary is a very good negotiating strategy because it resists appeals to reason. Let's look back at our example where the buyer has set an arbitrary upper price limit of $325,000 to better understand how this works. Let's also now assume that the seller has an appraisal on the property of $360,000. In a rational negotiation, the appraisal would be a strong indicator of the property's true worth and the seller could reasonably argue that the price should be in this range. However, when an arbitrary limit has been set the true worth of the property is of little relevance. The seller can explain why the higher price may be appropriate or fair until they are blue in the face. But at the end of the day, if the buyer sticks to her guns, the seller has to decide if she is willing to sell at that price. This confirms the point that there is nothing which requires a party to be either appropriate or fair in the negotiation. It's hard to negotiate against a brick wall!

How does one negotiate with someone who has set an arbitrary limit? There are two approaches. The first is to explain that the limit the party has set will simply not result in a deal being struck, but if party #1 reconsiders her position in the future, party #2 will be glad to re-open the negotiations. The second, and more challenging approach is to try to get the party being arbitrary to explain the basis of the arbitrary position they have set to see if reason can cause them to rethink their position. If a party has arbitrarily set a price limit for a new home at $325,00 and no houses meeting their needs are available in that price range, reason can often be used to cause the buyer to either set a higher price limit or look for a different type of house. (The challenge with this approach is that the parties who are arbitrary tend to be the same ones who are less than willing to reveal the bases for their position.)

If your clients understand that it is not their "job" to be either fair or reasonable, but to work with you to obtain the best price for the home they are buying or selling, you should be able to use arbitrary guidelines when it suits this purpose and your clients will not be surprised by such an approach.

Having given your clients an overview of the negotiation process itself, it's time to establish your game plan – to get specific about just where you want this negotiation to go. That's the subject of our next chapter.

Chapter 7

ESTABLISHING YOUR GAME PLAN

There's an old saying that if you don't know where you're going, you'll probably end up somewhere else. An appropriate paraphrase for the real estate professional might be: if you don't understand your client's needs and goals, you're likely not to meet them. It is important for you to determine just what your client's goals and expectations are, and to do so early in your relationship with them.

The main areas that need to be clarified are: (1) your client's expectations of you and the services you will be providing; (2) your expectations of your client and how you can together make an effective team; (3) the client's overall goals; (4) expectations on pricing; and (5) the limitations of your role as a negotiator. As you come to understand what they expect of you and exactly what their goals are, it becomes easier for you to help them reach their destination. As they come to understand better how they can help you, what the limitations of your role are, and what they can reasonably expect in terms of pricing (whether as seller or buyer), they will be more prepared for and more comfortable with the entire process.

Clarify Your Client's Expectations of You

The authors have defended literally thousands of claims brought against real estate agents. Sometimes the claims are deserved. More often the problem is not that the agent violated any law or that they necessarily did something wrong. The issue most frequently driving the claim is that the agent failed to meet her client's expectations. Think about it. If a transaction does not work out, but the client feels that the agent did everything expected of them, the client is very unlikely to blame the failed transaction on the agent.

These issues should be brought up at the very beginning of the relationship.

As agent, you can pre-empt the issue of failed expectations if you clarify what you plan to do for the client up front. Then ask your clients what their expectations are of you. Ask follow-up questions to general answers such as "we expect you to do a good job" or "we expect you to work hard." These are givens. Of course the client expects you to work hard and do a good job. The real questions are what does the client consider a "good job" or "hard work" to be? When representing a seller how many open houses does the client expect you to hold and when? What advertisement is expected? How many showings does the seller client expect? For buyer clients, how many houses does the buyer expect to be shown and how soon? How many houses at a time does the client expect you to show them? To some people, seeing three houses a week is plenty. Others may want you to spend the entire weekend showing them property. Finally, get the clients' agreement that what you are proposing to do is sufficient, or hopefully, above and beyond what they expected.

A criticism of real estate agents is that they put their own financial interests ahead of the interests of their clients. This same criticism is made of lawyers but in a slightly different way. Because lawyers often bill on an hourly basis, they are occasionally accused of looking for ways to increase the number of hours they spend on a matter. Since real estate agents often get a percentage of the sale price as their fee, the perception is that the agent is not as interested in getting the best price for the buyer or seller as spending the least amount of time needed to produce the greatest financial return to the agent.

Knowing that some may have concerns about your motivations, it is always best to address these types of issues head on. Not addressing these issues can be like sitting in a room with an elephant whose presence no one acknowledges. Unaddressed questions about an agent's motivations, and her commitment to the client, make it hard for clients to talk with their agents or to trust them. Discussing the issues up front is usually the best way to get them behind you and establish the credibility needed to be effective.

Tell the client that so long as their expectations are reasonable you will invest whatever time it takes to help them buy or sell a home at the very best price. They should also be reminded that since you only get paid if they buy or sell a home, they should be committed to the process and to you as their agent. Let the client know that you take the long-range view of your role, that you are interested not only in negotiating the best deal for them right now, but would like to develop a long-term relationship with them. A successful agent's clientele is primarily comprised of repeat customers and any clients they refer. It's the reality of the marketplace. It's honest. And being up front about it will reinforce your client's trust in you.

Clarify Your Expectations of Your Client

Remember that for most clients the buying or selling of a home is a rare occurrence. Your clients are stepping into unfamiliar territory, and will feel most comfortable if they have a handle on what will be expected of them in the process. Real estate agents know that the selling of any property is the result of combined efforts on the part of the seller and the agent. Be sure your client understands that it is a team effort, and just what things they can do to strengthen the likelihood of a "win."

Buying clients need to know that there are actions they can take that will help you to get the best price for a home they are interested in buying. Similarly, when you are the listing agent, make your client aware that there are actions they can take to draw more positive responses from agents and prospective buyers who view their home and ultimately to sell it at a higher price. The seller's responsibility will be to "stage" their home properly for showing such as presenting a clean and neat home and yard, minimizing clutter, keeping draperies open, etc.. (Entire books are written on this subject, and we will not go into detail here.) Suffice it to say that the better you prepare your clients for this aspect of the selling process, the shorter that process is likely to be.

Clarify the Client's Goals

While getting the best price is usually the stated goal of most buyers and sellers, there are often other interrelated goals which can be of equal or greater importance. Location and timing are the two most common. Examples of location goals for a buyer include the following:
• Owning a home in a particular school district
• Living close to a certain medical facility
• Living near relatives
• Living away from relatives
• Living close to work
• Being in a particular city or county
• Living near the water or golf course, or
• Living on a particular street or in a particular subdivision.

Examples of timing goals for a buyer include:
• Being in a home before the start of school
• Selling quickly because of a divorce or financial setback
• Closing within the time constraints of a 1031 like-kind
  exchange, and
• Locking in on a low interest rate loan.

There are also other specific goals and needs regarding the type of
house for which a buyer is looking. You might hear a client say:
• We really want to live in an older home with lots of charm
  and character.
• I can't climb stairs and need to live in a one story home.
• I cook a lot and need a big kitchen.
• We have 4 dogs and need a fenced yard and 'mud room.'
• We only want new construction, or
• I have children and do/do not want a pool.

Great negotiators learn to ask their buyer clients lots of questions
to help them better understand and define what it is they want.
They focus on their clients' verbal and non-verbal cues to gain
insight. They encourage clients to go through the "what would
you like more" or "which would you rather have" process in order
to help them prioritize. They ask them to list "must have,"
"would be nice to have," and "in my dreams I would have" features about the home they are looking for. They look for clues,
such as subtle changes of tone in a conversation, to pick up on
what dynamics are really at work.

You might consider developing a standardized interview sheet for
use with all prospective buyers. It could be a one- or two-page
form that guides you through some of these questions. Such an
interview sheet could be very useful later in providing a convenient summary of your client's goals.

Defining goals becomes even more complicated when representing multiple clients such as a husband and wife. The clients sometimes have completely different goals, or they may have the same goals but prioritize them differently. Extraneous factors such as how much sleep a client had the night before, how well the two clients are getting along, how their children are behaving, or how work went the day before can all influence their ability to define or voice what they want. Great negotiators, while following the lead of the client, also learn to gently bring them back to center or encourage them to reassess if they begin to stray too far.

Of course sellers have various goals as well, although most frequently it will be as direct as getting the best price for their home within what they consider a reasonable time frame. "Reasonable" is another one of those terms that needs to be explained – ask them just what that means for them. Be sure to clarify with your clients whether there are any specific time restrictions that will affect them, such as a previously scheduled relocation to another state, closing on a sale after the close of the school year, a divorce, death in the family, or financial setback. They may have financial considerations that dictate a firm bottom line in their price, or they may not be in any particular hurry at all.

Avoid becoming frustrated as goals change. Purchasing or selling real estate differs from most other personal sales transactions in one major respect. It is one of the few times when, at least in the traditional model, the buyer and seller hire someone else (you) to negotiate for them. While the negotiator must always defer to the stated wishes of the client, great negotiators accept and anticipate the fluid nature of the goal-setting process when representing someone else. Stated goals change. Goals sometimes come into conflict with one another. Choices may have to be made that result in goal modification or priority shuffling. Some clients don't want to share their goals, even though the information helps their agent-negotiator. Or clients may say their goals are one thing but later they turn out to be something else entirely. Knowing this from the start will help you keep your cool, and help you keep your clients on track through these changes.

Be sure to make notes of your clients' stated goals and check in with them from time to time if you see clues that goals may have shifted. Stay on the same page as your clients.

Establish Realistic Expectations on Pricing

Once you have identified your client's needs and goals, it's time to help them set realistic expectations regarding the type/price of property they seek, or regarding the property they wish to sell. This is definitely one of the most difficult tasks of a real estate agent, requiring skill and tact. Sellers tend to think their properties are worth more than they truly are. Buyers always think they will or should be able to get a better deal than everyone else in the market. Telling them about the market is simply not enough. Seeing is believing. If what a buyer client wants is not available at the price they want to pay, show them properties in their stated price range as well as properties with features that fit the description of what they want. Your job is to educate them on what is available and for what price. Likewise, if your seller's expectations are out of line, show them the other houses in a neighborhood against which their home is competing. While sellers may be uncomfortable shopping the competition, it is a time-tested tool to show them how their home stacks up in the market. Everyone's home may be their castle, but they may need to be gently told (and sometimes shown) if their home is more of a shack than a chateau.

The clients' expectations may not be in line with what you consider to be realistic. A seller, for instance, may think you should be able to sell their house for $750,000 even though you know that the property is worth, at most, $500,000. Some agents might be inclined to take the listing at the overvalued price thinking they will try and talk the seller into adjusting it after they have secured the listing. This is very shortsighted and sets the agent up for failure. The agent has allowed the seller to proceed with expectations that are not likely to be met. When this happens the seller is likely to blame the agent. Even if the seller later adjusts her expectations, the beneficiary is normally the second broker hired by the seller after the first one has been fired.

The better approach with clients is to make sure that they have realistic expectations from the start. Try to educate them about the likely sale price. Shop the competition with them. If at the end of the day they still want to list at $750,000, make them acknowledge that you think the price is too high. Make a deal with them that they agree to adjust the price if there are no offers after an agreed upon period of time.

Another option to consider at this point is "price range marketing." It is an option that may be used instead of setting a fixed asking price for a property. A home valued at $405,000, for example, might be listed "in a price range of $380,000 to $425,000." The hope of proponents of this approach is that the property will be exposed to more potential buyers, including prospects who would not even have looked at a property with a listing price of $405,000. (One agent described this as "fishing with a net compared with a single hook.") The tactic may indeed offer that advantage. The more prospects you have, the higher the likelihood that the property will sell quickly. In that case you may even be able to attract multiple offers simultaneously, conceivably putting your client in a very enviable position. If your seller is most interested in a quick sale you may want to discuss this option.

However, the tactic can also have its downside. With a "price range" approach the seller is not likely to receive any offers at the higher end of the range, unless a bidding war develops between multiple prospective buyers. Consider the pluses and minuses of this approach, and discuss them thoroughly with the seller before making a recommendation.

Limitations on the Negotiator

Clients need to know that no matter how good a negotiator you may be, you will not always be successful on their behalf. The people with whom we negotiate are not obligated to be fair or even rational. Lawyers often joke that if everyone was rational, told the truth, and always did what they are supposed to do, then lawyers would need to find a new line of work!

You can do your best for your client, but there's no way to ever guarantee a particular result. There are sellers' markets and buyers' markets. There is supply and demand. There is emotion versus logic. All of these factors can impact the relative bargaining power of the parties. The authors know a builder who will only use his own contract containing the most onerous, one-sided, unfair provisions we have ever seen. A real estate agent correctly identified that his buyer client should exercise caution with this builder's contract. He sent the client to one of the authors for a legal consultation regarding the contract terms. We did everything we could to warn the buyer that it was, in our opinion, unwise to enter into this contract. We went back to the builder countless times trying to negotiate more buyer-friendly terms in the contract. At the end of the day the builder said he would just sell to someone else if the buyer did not like his contract. The builder had an exclusive right to build in the subdivision, and the buyer was adamant about living there. So, despite all the agent and we lawyers could do, the builder got his way.

Be mindful of the limitations of your role as well, and avoid confusing your goals with those of your client. One of the biggest mistakes negotiators make is to substitute their own judgment for that of their client. At the end of the day it doesn't matter whether you think a particular deal is good or not. It's what your client thinks that counts. If a buyer overpays but gets her dream home, that buyer may have achieved her goal.

We know what you're thinking. Wouldn't it have been even better if the buyer got the house of her dreams without having to overpay for it? While this is certainly true, where would the client be if she lost the house to another buyer because the negotiator was too focused on her own priorities, such as pushing for a lower price, rather than those of the client? In such a case the negotiator has failed. It is fine to let the client know that you think they are not getting the best deal possible. However, if at the end of the day they want to purchase at a higher price or sell for less than you think they should, it is your job to complete the deal at that price.

You've done your homework. You know the general market conditions and the neighborhood in which your client is planning to buy or sell. Your client's expectations of you and the process have been addressed, and your client is prepared to begin. What can you do at this stage to prepare yourself more fully? Our next chapter will tell you the answer.

Chapter 8

PERSPECTIVE, PRACTICE AND PEP TALKS

There are three things that every sports team includes in the preparation for game day - having the right perspective on what's at stake, engaging in sufficient practice to prepare physically, and hearing a good pep talk from the coach to fire them up mentally. With real estate negotiation you are both a player and the coach, so all of these aspects of preparation are on your shoulders.

Perspective

First, it is important for real estate professionals to remember that they are negotiating on someone else's behalf. This means that whether the agent is successful or not in the negotiation is not so much a matter of how well the agent thinks she did, but instead how well the client thinks the agent did. There may be times when a buyer or seller is unhappy with the result of the negotiation when in reality the agent may have negotiated very well on the client's behalf. Similarly, there may be times when an agent is disappointed with how well she did in the negotiation, yet the client is quite pleased with the outcome. The client's perception is as important as the reality. Therefore, the agent must focus on the negotiation from the client's perspective and keep the client fully informed of its progress. Communication is key to having a satisfied client. And satisfied clients are key to having a successful real estate business.

Second, since more buyers and sellers are now being represented by agents working with them in a client capacity, negotiations can be fairly complex as we have mentioned before. In many of these negotiations there are one or two buyers, one or two sellers, one or two real estate agents, friends and family members giving advice, and a variety of inspectors – all giving input on what they believe the terms of the transaction should be. These potentially complex dynamics demonstrate the need to become an expert in the negotiation process. Real estate agents need their voice to be the voice of wisdom, experience, and expertise. While it may not necessarily be the loudest voice in the room, the goal of the real estate agent should be that her voice is the one clients hear above all the others and listen to most closely.

Third, unlike many negotiations, the livelihood of the negotiator in a real estate transaction is tied to a successful outcome. If a person goes to buy a new car and the negotiations do not go well, the worst thing that happens is that she either doesn't buy a car or pays too much. When real estate negotiations don't go well the credibility and financial well being of the agent are on the line. While agents want to help their clients achieve their goals, agents have a vested interest in keeping the negotiation on track and seeing it through to a successful conclusion. Keeping this in mind will help a real estate professional retain a sharp focus.

Practice, Practice, Practice

Having at least some oral advocacy skills is helpful to being a good negotiator. But whether you have strong advocacy skills or not, part of the art of negotiation is preparing yourself in advance, behind the scenes. Some people are just naturally quick on their feet. Most of us, however, can appear to be quick on our feet if we have mastered the subject matter in advance of the negotiation and think through the likely questions, responses, follow-up questions and follow-up responses. Being prepared really is the best way to give you an edge. Visualize the negotiation in advance. Ask yourself, "What questions might I be asked? What objections might be raised? How will I respond? How can I structure the give-and-take to achieve the goal?"

Even the experts practice to make themselves better. One trick that John Roberts, now Chief Justice of the United States Supreme Court, used when he was arguing cases before the Supreme Court was to write down each of the questions he might be asked about a case on 3 x 5 cards. He would then randomly mix the cards and practice making a coherent argument regardless of the order in which the questions were asked.

For real estate agents the first negotiation is often not between a seller and a prospective buyer. It is between the agent and the prospective client at the listing presentation. Let's imagine that you are going on a listing presentation to the house of a seller who indicated over the phone that she is also considering a discount broker. Obviously, she is considering a very different business model and wants to pay you less money than what you want to charge. So, you are headed into your first negotiation and the house is not even listed! How do you visualize the negotiation with such a seller?

The best way to prepare for this or any other negotiation is to write down what you believe the main argument of the other side (in this case, the prospective seller) is going to be and then all of the counter arguments you might make in response to the those points. Review your different arguments and rate them as weak, strong or average. Put yourself in the seller's position, and imagine what objections or additional follow-up questions may be raised and address those as well. Come up with ways to turn average arguments into strong ones. Practice making your presentation, starting with what you believe is your strongest point. Let's walk through this process together, using the following example.

Let's assume that a seller is considering hiring you or a discount broker. The seller will likely be arguing the standard line for this approach, which would be something like this:

> *"Look, as I told you, I'm also considering a discount broker age firm. It looks like the main part of getting any house sold is to get it listed in a multiple listing service and expose it to as broad a market of buyers as possible. Since others are charging $500 for this service, why should I pay you a 6% commission on the entire sale price?"*

The seller is basically saying that the main part of selling a home is getting it listed in a multiple listing service; and they want you, the listing agent, to cut your fee if you want their business. You need to explain that she is comparing apples to oranges. Explain why your services as a traditional listing agent are different and better than those a discount broker offers, and why you therefore can't or won't reduce your commission.

You might make the following types of arguments:

> *ARGUMENT 1: My fee is more than a discount broker's fee, but I will also be providing significantly more service, with better results, than will a discount broker. The marketing services I offer, and that we covered a few minutes ago, will expose your property to a larger group of prospective buyers, increasing the likelihood that your home will sell more quickly and at a higher price.*
>
> RATING: STRONG

Limited-service brokers largely list property in a multiple listing service or on web sites which often are not state of the art. While such advertising exposes property to a broad audience of potential buyers, many homes are sold through other means including newspaper and magazine advertising, elaborate brochures, advertising on television, sharing with other agents (who have prospective buyers of their own) that the property is available, including the property in "agent caravans," holding open houses, doing an agent lunch at the home, and distributing fliers describing the property to homes and to business, religious, cultural and educational institutions in the surrounding neighborhood.

Traditional agents can offer more intensive marketing than most discount brokers, often resulting in a quicker sale. Selling a house faster can mean thousands of dollars of savings to the seller, more than recouping for them the cost of the commission. This argument establishes one big advantage against limited-service brokers: that you, the traditional broker, are in a position to help your client get a much better deal than they could either on their own or with the discount broker.

> *ARGUMENT 2: The biggest variable in the amount of money a seller makes in selling her home is not the commission which is paid but the price at which the house is sold. As a trained negotiator, I can help you get the highest price for your home.*
>
> RATING: STRONG

There are two parts to this argument. The first is that the agent has the negotiation skills to help the seller get a better price for his home. The second is that this may result in the seller netting far more than if the property is listed with a discount broker.

Convincing the seller that you have good negotiation skills is not necessarily easy. Many sellers see themselves as good negotiators. What you say here will obviously depend on your background and training. You are only as good a negotiator as your expertise with the product for which you are negotiating. (Remember our discussion about buying a car?) An agent trained as a negotiator brings a combination of knowledge of how to negotiate and a special familiarity with the market.

The second part of this argument is the economic analysis of the ultimate selling price of the home, and the real financial impact of the difference in services. (See Chapter 3 for a detailed discussion.)

> ARGUMENT 3: *Discount brokers cost more than you might think.*
>
> RATING: AVERAGE

The advertisements of most limited-service brokerage firms focus on the small amount paid to the listing agent. This gets your property listed in a multiple listing service. However, with most discount brokerage models, the seller still pays a commission or a percentage of the sale price to the selling agent. In addition, sellers will have to pay extra to get the listing agent to advise them and negotiate on their behalf.

Thus far this is only an "average" argument. How can it be strengthened? At this point your preparation will pay off. By knowing in advance what types of fee structures discount brokers are offering in your area, you can know exactly how to make the comparison relevant and concrete to the seller. Go through the specific numbers. The financial disparity between the two models can be reversed in your favor as you highlight the likely economic outcome to your prospect.

NEW RATING: STRONG

ARGUMENT 4: Most agents working for discount brokers are inexperienced; therefore, their knowledge of contracts, pricing and negotiation skills are very limited.

RATING: WEAK

Don't criticize the competition. It can backfire. As a wise old attorney said, "If the only way to get business is to knock the competition, the cost to your character of getting the business may be too great."

ARGUMENT 5: My experience allows me more creative ways to sell your property. The knowledge I bring to the negotiation table with any prospective buyer enables me to get the best possible price for you. For serious sellers, the cheapest option is not usually the best option.

RATING: STRONG

This argument is the opposite of the previous argument. Rather than knocking the competition to try to get business, the focus of the argument is on the skills and experience of the agent in being able to get the property sold. People love a winner who exudes confidence. When an agent can confidently state her qualifications, that alone can be a powerful argument.

ARGUMENT 6: My broker won't allow me to reduce my commission.

RATING: WEAK

Although it is possibly true, it "passes the buck." It can also give your prospective client a negative perception of your broker and lessen your standing.

ARGUMENT 7: When buyers see a property that is listed with a discount broker, they often offer less money for the property.

RATING: AVERAGE

Some sellers think they save money by listing with a discount broker. However, many savvy buyers have told us that if a property is listed as for sale by owner or with a discount broker, they will offer less money than if it is listed with a traditional broker. If buyers automatically reduce their offer by the amount they think a broker would charge, then sellers may actually save nothing by using a discount broker.

This argument is rated as "average" because it is something of a double-edged sword. Some sellers will believe that they can outsmart the buyer to capture the savings for themselves. Others may decide it's okay if the buyer gets a better deal because there will then be more prospective buyers for the property.

ARGUMENT 8: Full-service agents only get paid if your house is sold, and are paid more if they sell your house for a higher price. Therefore, I have a built-in incentive to get you the best possible price for your home, unlike a discount broker whose flat fee is paid regardless of success or failure and regardless of what a final sale price might be.

RATING: STRONG

A point which is often lost on sellers is that discount brokers get paid the flat fee regardless of whether or not they sell the home. Where is their incentive to work for the client? Commissioned real estate agents only get paid if they sell your home. Agents do not emphasize enough that all of their work is negated if they do not find a buyer for the property. When there is a risk of getting paid nothing, the reward for success should always be higher.

> *ARGUMENT 9. If a discount broker immediately cuts her price down to the absolute minimum, how do you think the discounter will do negotiating a price for your home?*
> RATING: WEAK

This argument "turns the tables" on the premise of the limited-service broker model. It should serve as a reminder to a seller that you get what you pay for. However, it's a "knock-the-competition" type of argument and negative arguments often backfire.

So you are left with several strong arguments, and you have bolstered the average arguments. (Of course, just discard the weak ones.) Think about the follow-up arguments the seller might make in response to your arguments, and how you might respond. Then it's time to practice your responses (out loud if possible) until they start to become second nature to you. This is a great exercise to do while you're driving. (Just pretend that you are having a hands-free conversation with someone on the cell phone so that your neighbors in traffic don't think you are talking to yourself!) Practice presenting your arguments in different ways, and in different order. This will help you gain confidence in your ability to demonstrate your negotiation skills to the prospective client. The point is that when you are prepared for a negotiation you may not win, but you will rarely be left flat-footed.

Pep Talks

Once all of your practicing is finished it's time to get mentally prepared for the main event. The old "win one for the Gipper" pep-talk takes on a different form for the agent preparing for a negotiation. Just as professional athletes go through game day rituals and routines to build their confidence or to "psych" themselves up for the big game, negotiators need to do the same thing. If you are going on a listing call where you know you will be negotiating your commission, wear an article of clothing that brings you good luck or in which you feel particularly comfortable and confident. Talk to yourself about being confident in the negotiation. Visualize yourself succeeding in the negotiation. Listen to music that will "get your juices flowing." Drink a cup of coffee to give yourself a caffeine boost. Negotiations require you to be alert and at the top of your game. Do what works for you.

One thing that makes being a good real estate negotiator more difficult than being, for example, a professional athlete, is that you don't always know when the game will be played. You can on occasion receive a phone call from another agent and suddenly find yourself in the middle of an important negotiation you had not expected. With some advance thought you can control much more of the action than you think. If the ball is in your court, you can decide when to make a critical phone call, send an important fax, or schedule a key meeting. If the ball is in the other party's court, anticipate when they might call you. Know the other agent's phone number and have "caller ID" on your phone (or enter it into your cell phone) to minimize the likelihood of being surprised. Again, do what works for you.

Remember: this is the skill for which you are now being paid the big bucks.

The suggestions we make in the next section are primarily for use in the actual negotiations for a property. What we've already covered does not lose its importance. Negotiation is not an event –

it is a process. Know the property. Know the market. Know your client and her goals. And keep your knowledge updated about those areas as the process unfolds. Now, let's move on to the main event.

PART III

GAME TIME:
RULES FOR
SUCCESSFUL
NEGOTIATORS

Chapter 9

RULES FOR ROOKIES

There are of course the official "rules of the game," the legal and ethical requirements placed on real estate professionals by federal, state and local authorities. These are not the subject of this chapter or of this book. What we mean here by "rules" are some tried and true guidelines that will help you in any negotiation. They are approaches to take, bits of wisdom to remember – the tools you will use as needed to fine-tune the process as it goes along. They may be applied somewhat differently in various negotiating situations, but the guidelines themselves will remain. One thing to keep in mind about the rules we will present in this book: while they will definitely help you become a better negotiator, how and when they are used will be for each negotiator to decide. Negotiators need to experiment until they discover what works best for them.

Real estate negotiation is a bit like playing blackjack. No, we don't mean that it's always a gamble. For those of you who are unfamiliar with this card game, let me explain what we mean. In blackjack there are well-known rules for when you take a card and when you do not. Any good blackjack player will tell you that over time, following the rules will mathematically produce better results for the card player than not following them. Of course, this does not guarantee that if you follow the rules you will beat the dealer every time. The same principal holds true for our rules and real estate negotiation. There will be times when you will follow the rules outlined in this book and still end up with an unsuccessful result in the negotiation. There are so many variables in a negotiation there can be no guarantees. But we know from experience that following our rules over time will produce better results for you in your negotiations.

What things should you do or not do to maximize the likelihood of success? We have several suggestions for rules you may want to adopt in your negotiations. Our first examples (we refer to as Rules for Rookies) are the basics, the things every agent should know and practice in any negotiation. We have five "DOs" and five "DON'Ts for you to apply.

The DO List

RULE NO. 1   BE OBSERVANT

One of the authors recently helped a family member buy a new home in Atlanta. The property had originally been listed for $1,100,000 (in a neighborhood of much more expensive homes) and had subsequently been reduced to $995,000. In walking through the house, the author (our Mr. X) noticed a couple of rooms which, while they still contained furniture, looked somewhat bare. The house also looked a little worn around the edges.

As the prospective purchasers (relatives of Mr. X) walked through the house, Mr. X struck up a conversation with the listing agent who happened to also be the mother of the seller. They discussed their respective families, where they were from, whether she was having a good year in real estate, and eventually Mr. X worked his way around to asking how motivated her daughter was and why she was selling. The listing agent's initial reaction was one of surprise. How did Mr. X know the seller was her daughter? He pointed to several photographs of the owner on a coffee table, snapshots that included the agent. (Remember item number 30 in Chapter 6? Be on the lookout for subtle hints and clues about the other party to the transaction.) Our Mr. X then asked, "I don't mean to pry, but is your daughter going through a divorce?" When the agent asked how Mr. X knew that, he politely said that it looked like about half of the furniture in the home had been removed. The agent quickly opened up and confided that her daughter had recently gone through a divorce and needed to sell the property.

As a courtesy to the listing agent, Mr. X called her back the next day to let her know that while his sister-in-law liked the house her husband did not, and that they were going to continue their search. Her disappointment was palpable. In a cracking voice she explained that her daughter needed to sell quickly and that she had been hoping Mr. X's relatives would buy the house.

Knowing that a good deal could likely be had on the house, Mr. X told her that he occasionally bought houses as investments, fixed them up and resold them. Mr. X truthfully told the listing agent that he would be willing to pay $900,000 for the house. Two days later, the seller accepted the offer (which Mr. X later learned was $50,000 less than the seller had paid for the property two years earlier). When Mr. X's relatives learned of the good deal he had gotten on the house they decided they really did like it after all and Mr. X assigned them the contract.

There are several lessons to be learned from this example. The first is that the person with whom you are negotiating usually responds more positively when you are friendly. Second, careful observation is revealing. The author knew that: (1) this was one of the least expensive homes in the neighborhood; (2) most buyers were either looking for new homes or homes which did not need the amount of work this home needed; and (3) had this home been updated, the seller would likely have gotten a higher price to offset the cost of the updates. A seller whose primary focus is obtaining the highest possible price would have put some money into the property to get it ready for showing. Because this was not done Mr. X knew the seller was more interested in a quick sale than the best price.

RULE NO. 2   BE FRIENDLY

Being successful in business is all about forming relationships. And negotiation is all about relationships and compromise. In many cultures people will not even begin to consider doing business together until they have spent a sufficient period of time socializing and getting to know one another. While this may appear quaint to some, there is a logical purpose to this prelude to business. It allows the parties to assess with whom they are dealing and to decide if they want to do business together. Judging from the large amount of litigation which arises out of the purchase and sale of properties we could probably all take a lesson from, and do more to follow, this approach.

Forming relationships requires people to be friendly and accommodating. When one person likes the person with whom they are negotiating they are usually more willing to open up and compromise. The same applies to real estate agents negotiating with one another on behalf of their clients. If one agent dislikes the other agent or that agent's principal they are less likely to recommend that their client make or agree to concessions sought by the other party. The phrase "you can catch more flies with honey than you can with vinegar" has great applicability to negotiations.

Here's how it works. The seller generally does not meet the buyer until the closing. Most sellers, however, form an image in their minds about buyers and whether they like them. Their perception is somewhat based upon the terms of the buyers' offer, and it is somewhat formed by their listing agent's description of the buyer and/or the buyer's agent. Thus, the buyer's agent becomes the buyer in the mind of the seller. If the seller is told by his agent that the buyer's agent acts like a jerk, the seller will naturally also think of the buyer as unlikable. We are known by the company we keep.

A common example of this involves two buyers competing to buy the same house. When buyers make offers which are generally equal it is usually the nicer buyer or the buyer whose agent is more agreeable who ends up with the property. Some sellers, particularly those who have lived in their home a long time, want their property to go to a buyer whom they or their agents view as nice or with whom they otherwise connect. If the buyer's agent acts poorly the listing agent is often influenced to have a negative view of both the buying agent and her client.

We have seen real estate transactions in which a seller gave buyer # 1, whom they liked, an opportunity to match the offer of buyer # 2, whom they did not like. As attorneys, we have twice seen a buyer of commercial property lose a deal because the buyer's attorney had been unprofessional in a transaction unrelated to the buyer. The seller refused to work with the attorney because of the earlier experience. As a result, the buyer never had a chance. This confirms the perception that the sins of an agent are often visited upon the agent's principal.

RULE NO. 3   BE CURIOUS

Now armed with all of your observations and a friendly demeanor, be prepared to ask lots of questions as well as to respond to them. If you keep getting the wrong answer in your negotiations, it could be because you are asking the wrong questions. This rule comes into play throughout the negotiation process, but particularly in the "pre-game" period when clients are deciding whether to enter into full-scale negotiations.

The types of questions we will be suggesting should never be asked in rapid-fire succession. You are not conducting an interrogation, after all, but wanting to maintain a friendly atmosphere for the negotiation. The questions should be casually interwoven into a much longer conversation.

What kinds of questions should the agent representing a buyer ask? Our suggestions:

Questions to ask the Listing Agent
• Who owns the property?
• How long has the seller owned the property?
• Does the seller still reside in the property?
• Has the seller made any major improvements to the property? If so, what are they?
• Why is the seller selling?
• Does the seller have any special needs (e.g., a need for a quick or delayed sale)?
• How motivated is the seller to sell the property?
• How long has the property been on the market?
• Has the property been under contract before? If so, why did the previous contract fall through?

These questions can indicate to a real estate agent a seller's motivation and if there is a good deal to be had on the property. The same holds true for agents representing the seller. Questions are equally important for a listing agent in a transaction. Some of the questions which would help a listing agent better understand the motivations of the buyer are as follows:

Questions to ask the Selling Agent
• Who is your buyer?
• Where is the buyer moving from? Where does the buyer now live?
• Is this the buyer's first house?
• Why are they looking for a new home?
• Is the move job related? If so, is the buyer's employer offering any incentives such as absorbing some of the closing costs?
• How long has the buyer been looking for a home?

- Where else are they looking?
- Is the buyer interested in any special features; i.e. a pool, or a full basement?
- Do they need to be in a new home by a particular date? Are there any special needs for a quick or delayed closing?
- Has the buyer made offers on other properties? If so, what happened?
- Have they been pre-qualified for a mortgage loan? If so, in what amount? By whom? Was the pre-approval based on a full credit check of the buyers?

We also recommend that the listing agent be present during all property visits. In some parts of the country listing agents tend not to be present during showings to allow the buyer's agent to show the property to their client on their own. While this may be a time saver for listing agents, it is a missed opportunity to evaluate the buyers and discern their motivations.

So far, we've covered lots of questions you should be asking. As a good negotiator, you should also anticipate questions from the other side. Try to identify questions that might harm your client's negotiation position and be ready for them. What do you do when you are on the receiving end of questions you do not want to answer for fear it will harm your client's negotiating position? (NOTE: It should be emphasized here that we are not talking about questions which must be answered to comply with the law; nor are we advocating a way of committing fraud. See Chapter 15 for a discussion of avoiding legal pitfalls). The answer is to do your homework, anticipate the questions that will likely be asked of you, and think through in advance what your answers will be. (The process we walked through in Chapter 8, practicing your arguments, can be useful here as well.)

For example, how might you respond to a question like, "Why is the seller selling the property?" Or, "Why has the buyer decided to relocate?" Consider giving a more noncommittal answer like, "My client has decided to downsize" as opposed to saying that your client is getting a divorce. It's still an honest answer, but there is no need for the other party to know the reason for the downsizing. Another acceptable response is to say, "My client is a private person and asked that I not disclose any personal information about her reasons," or "my client found a home in _____ that she is interested in buying," or "my client has put a house under contract in _____." It is also perfectly acceptable to say, "I'm not sure." All of these answers follow the time-honored approach of talking without saying anything. While perfecting this skill requires practice, the key elements are to smile a lot, say something general in response to the questions, and then move on to a different subject. (Watch C-SPAN for some great examples of this skill.)

It should be noted that many good negotiators intentionally say nothing (or say nothing and stare the other person in the eye) when the response to a question they have asked is not on point. Some people are uncomfortable with periods of silence in conversations. If the responding agent is one of those people and gives a somewhat unresponsive answer, she may look to fill the void with additional conversation and say something she did not intend to disclose. Don't let your discomfort with silence cause you to give unnecessary information.

You can also find out what the other person's tolerance is for silence, and discern how this might give you an edge. Test how well this works for you. Ask a seller sometime if she is aware of any defects in the property other than those she has already disclosed. If the seller says "no," simply stop talking for 10-15 seconds and look the seller in the eyes. See if they don't start talking about a defect they forgot to previously mention, or elaborate on some defect which they already disclosed. See how fast they start speaking to avoid the uncomfortable silence. Silence sometimes is truly golden, and is sometimes a weapon that can be used to actually glean additional information.

RULE NO. 4   BE PATIENT

Patience is a virtue – most of the time – and may be the most important skill of a great negotiator. It is also something that is in short supply when a buyer or seller is excited about the prospect of buying or selling a particular property. When most buyers or sellers make an offer to purchase or sell property they normally start wondering whether their offer will be accepted within a couple of hours. While wondering is fine, calling is not. Buyer agents regularly report that they know the buyer is on the hook when the buyer starts calling them within an hour or so after making an offer wondering if the agent has heard from the other side.

Part of being patient involves waiting a reasonable period of time before responding to an offer. One of the authors recently finished a negotiation for a developer client who was eager to get a $30 million apartment building (that he was going to convert to a condominium) under contract. The negotiations were protracted and intense. The first time the seller made a counteroffer the buyer called the author and said, "Call the seller back right away. Let him know I'll increase my offer but only to $_____." The author called a time-out and tried to slow his client down as best he could. If the seller had been called with a counteroffer within ten minutes of the buyer receiving the seller's offer, the message the seller would clearly have received was that the buyer was chomping at the bit to get this property under contract. While there are occasions where this may be the message the buyer wants to give the seller, expressing such keen interest comes at a price - usually a higher one than the buyer might otherwise have to pay for the property.

Sometimes the best way to succeed at a negotiation with a motivated seller or buyer is to use patience to an extreme and to simply do nothing. We've seen many transactions in which the seller makes a counteroffer only to find the buyer not respond with another offer. If the buying agent reports that the buyer is considering the seller's last offer but is also looking at other properties, and if the seller has no other interested buyers, the seller may bid against herself and make a lower offer to keep negotiations open. If a seller makes an additional offer in this situation, it is obviously a strong signal to the buyers that there are no other active prospects looking to purchase.

Of course, patience can work for both sides. If your seller client is in a strong bargaining position (due to market conditions or time constraints of the buyer for example), doing nothing may be the best move. Conversely, in slow housing markets buyers (being in short supply) have superior bargaining power. A buyer can use a go-slow strategy very effectively to win concessions from the seller because the seller has little choice but to try to make a deal with any one of the precious few buyers in the market. However, if the seller has other viable options to sell the property, a slow response from a buyer can be interpreted as disinterest.

Clients and their agents sometimes inadvertently tip their hand (and true level of interest) by appearing impatient. Let's look at the following example: Seller has his house listed for $500,000 with Broker Sally. Buyer is represented by Broker Bob. Buyer makes a low offer to purchase the property at $440,000 in a strong real estate market. The offer is open for acceptance for 3 days. At the end of the second day, Broker Bob starts calling Broker Sally. When they connect, Sally and Bob have the following conversation:

BROKER BOB	Hi, Sally. I was just calling to make sure you'd received my offer.
BROKER SALLY	Yes, I received your offer and forwarded it on to my sellers yesterday morning.
BROKER BOB	Oh, that's good. I hadn't heard from you so I wasn't sure. Have you heard from them? I like to keep my clients fully informed about what's going on in the transaction.
BROKER SALLY	No, I haven't. Your clients gave them 3 days to decide. I don't yet know their response.
BROKER BOB	Let me know when you hear.
BROKER SALLY	Okay, I'll do that. Good-bye.

If you are the agent representing the seller, what could you conclude about this conversation? The initial statement made by Broker Bob is not believable. If Bob was really calling to confirm that the offer was received, why wait until the end of the second day to inquire about it? More than likely Broker Bob would have called immediately upon delivering the offer. Most negotiators would interpret this as the buyer having more interest in the house than the low offer would indicate. The call indicates an expression of interest and possibly some anxiety on the part of the buyer about losing the house to another buyer. Based on the phone call some savvy sellers would counter at a price higher than they might have had no phone call been made. Why? Because of the buyer agent's lack of patience.

While patience is important, there may also be reasons to limit the time frame of an offer or counteroffer. The seller could have received two good offers on a property at the same time. In countering one of the offers, the seller may need to leave his counteroffer open for only a short period so as not to lose buyer #2 if buyer #1 rejects the counteroffer. In such situations, it is usually best to communicate why a short time frame is being given. If there is not a good reason for the limited time, the buyer may react negatively to the seller's time-limited offer.

A short period of time to accept or reject an offer without good reason is a high stakes form of negotiating. Such an offer will on occasion be accepted. However, there is a greater likelihood that it will be rejected. Again, patience is necessary for both sides. An offer accepted too quickly can leave the buyer wondering whether she could have gotten the property for less, particularly if a buyer's first offer is accepted.

Let's suppose that a seller lists his property for $549,000 but is really willing to accept $500,000. The buyer's initial offer is $516,000. If the seller immediately accepts this offer, some buyers will be thrilled but others would speculate that they overpaid. If this happens, some buyers may try to get out of the contract.

In this example the seller should either wait a few days to accept the buyer's offer or make a counteroffer $5,000 higher than the buyer's offer. The buyer may conclude the seller is making a concession in price and that the seller's bottom line price has now been revealed. If the deal is done both sides will likely feel like winners. And everyone likes to be a winner.

Be patient when you are negotiating. When you lose your patience, you usually lose.

RULE NO. 5   BE REASONABLE WHEN
SETTING TIME FRAMES

In any negotiation reasonable time frames must be established to insure that the negotiation proceeds at a reasonable pace for the protection of the parties and of the negotiation itself. As we have developed more and faster means of communication, the length of time an offer is open for acceptance has decreased. While everyone has their own thoughts on what is a reasonable time frame to leave an offer open for acceptance, we believe that one to three days is sufficient. It is also generally acceptable to shorten the length of time for successive counteroffers to remain open for acceptance as the parties progress through their negotiation.

If too long a time frame is given for a party to respond there is a greater chance that a competitor will emerge on the scene. For example, if a buyer offers $600,000 for a piece of property but leaves the offer open for 90 days, the seller now has the metaphorical "bird in the hand" and can search for the one in the bush. Known also as "shopping an offer," the seller can spread the word of the offer and indicate that any buyer who can top the offer wins the property. There are many who still believe that shopping an offer is unethical. Views on the ethics of this practice are changing. The National Association of REALTORS,® in its Code of Ethics, now takes the position that it is appropriate in certain circumstances to disclose the existence of other offers on a property. (See Standard of Practice 1-15, amended January 2006.) However, it is certainly a risky approach which, if discovered, can result in the withdrawal of the original offer.

Sellers who decide that shopping an offer is worth the risk should carefully consider whether or not to reveal the amount of the offer they have in hand. If the seller announces that she has received an offer of $600,000, the odds of any subsequent offer being significantly higher than that is not particularly great (i.e., expect no more than $610,000). However, if the amount of the offer in hand is not announced a subsequent offer may be either higher or lower than the offer on the table.

To some degree the decision as to whether to reveal the amount of a previous offer may depend on how long the seller has to shop the offer. If the seller has plenty of time the best strategy is to withhold the amount of the offer in hand. If the seller has only a short time, revealing the amount of the offer in hand may hasten the process of getting another buyer to come forward with a higher offer.

The Don't Do List

RULE NO. 6   DON'T SWEAT THE SMALL STUFF

It is amazing when negotiations collapse over disputes of a few hundred dollars. Common are the seller's refusal to pay for carpet cleaning or a buyer's insistence that a refrigerator remain with the property. A dispute over $500 is inconsequential when compared to a home priced in the hundreds of thousands of dollars. We often explain to buyers that when you amortize $500 over 30 years at a 6% interest rate it adds $3.00 per month to the cost of the house. That's 10 cents per day. Emotions – and egos – all too often kill a deal.

Both emotion and ego can enter the picture when a buyer or seller gets to the point where making one final concession becomes "the straw that breaks the camel's back" or is the one point that makes the client feel like they are going to "lose." The clients can begin to feel that they are the only side giving an inch, or that their pride can "only take so much." How can the real estate agent prevent this from occurring? There are a few things you can do in addition to explaining the economic realities of the cost of the disputed item amortized over the life of a mortgage.

First, before the negotiation actually begins, give your clients examples of transactions where this type of dispute arose. Explain how pride and fear can cause all of us to act a bit irrationally in the heat of the moment. Most clients will understand the illogic of letting a deal die over a few hundred dollars (particularly when the stories you use as examples involve clients other than themselves). If later in the negotiations the client becomes involved in a similar dispute of this type, reminding them of your earlier conversation may encourage them to act logically.

Another suggestion is to tell the client in advance to let you know when they are at least one concession away from the breaking point. If the client forgets to do so remind them of their promise and ask for patience. In many negotiations one party or the other will push for concessions until they are told no. If this doesn't happen they may push the negotiation too far, jeopardize their position, and then not know how to gracefully bring the negotiation back into safe territory.

A good negotiator lets the other side know when her client appears to be getting close to the breaking point. We tell the representative of another client that if the client really wants the property, she won't ask for one more thing because we can tell when our client is about to end negotiations and she's just about there. When parties on the other side hear this message most of them will take a step back and evaluate whether they can accept the deal as it stands. If they can, they will usually stop pushing – or at least not push too hard. If the deal is one they can live without the party may continue to ask for concessions, but does so knowing that dangerous territory is ahead.

RULE NO. 7   DON'T PUT YOUR COMMISSION IN
PLAY IN THE NEGOTIATION

How many times have you seen the following happen? A seller lists property for $500,000. An interested buyer comes along and makes a low offer. After a series of offers and counteroffers, the parties remain approximately $5,000 apart. At this point the seller turns to the listing agent and says, "I've gone down on my price as far as I'm willing to go. If you want this sale to happen, you will have to reduce your commission to make up the difference." Rather than representing the seller in a negotiation with the buyer you are now put in the position of negotiating with the seller over your commission. Sellers often do this to net a higher return. Enough listing agents agree to reduce their commissions that sellers continue to ask. (If you don't reduce your commission in response to this tactic and the deal falls apart, the seller will likely blame you.)

How do you prevent this from happening? We recommend that you discuss and agree on your commission with the client as part of the "behind the scenes action" when you are establishing your game plan with her. That's the time to emphasize that once the commission has been agreed to it is not something you will further change or reduce, and that it is not available for later re-negotiation. While this may sound a bit harsh, experience shows that there are fewer problems in a professional relationship when each party's expectations are clearly stated. If you are clear from the beginning that you will not reduce or negotiate your commission, it's less likely the seller will press you for a reduction later. Of course, once you have taken a firm stand on your commission do not back off. If you do, you are likely to lose credibility with your client.

RULE NO. 8   DON'T PAINT YOURSELF INTO
A CORNER

One of the mistakes buyers and sellers make is not leaving themselves any wiggle room in the negotiation. It is unrealistic to
expect people not to try to negotiate a better deal. Therefore,
leaving a little room to go higher or lower helps increase the likelihood of a successful outcome. Always leave some room for compromise.

While the amount of room left for compromise in a negotiation
is important, the pace at which the gap is closed between two perspective positions may be even more important. One of the big-
ger mistakes people make in negotiating is to leave room for compromise, but then try to close the gap in the first or second counteroffer. Let's say that a buyer is willing to pay $550,000 for a
property, but initially offers $500,000. If the seller, who had the
property listed at $599,000, counters at $589,000, it is not
uncommon for buyers to grow impatient and raise their offer to
$550,000. At this point the buyer has left herself no room for
further compromise. Moving from $500,000 to $550,000 is
obviously a big jump and may send a message that the buyer's first
offer was too low, rather than the buyer simply trying to wrap up
the deal. Such a big price jump should cause the seller to make a
significant further concession in the price at which she will sell the
property. However, a good negotiator will normally not agree to
meet the buyer's price, but will instead counter in the $565,000
to $570,000 range. If the buyer wants the property, odds are the
buyer will now have to offer $7,500 to $10,000 more to close the
deal.

The buyer's impatience in closing the gap too quickly may have
resulted in the buyer paying more for the property than she needed to. Had the buyer closed the gap over several counteroffers

there is a much better likelihood that the buyer would have gotten the property at a better price.

Leaving room to negotiate can also be over non-monetary items. For example, a buyer offers to increase the purchase price but only if the seller agrees to move up the closing date. This allows the buyer to lock in a better interest rate and save thousands of dollars over the term of the loan. Similarly, if a buyer hits a brick wall regarding the sale price, the buyer may ask for certain items to remain with the property, such as outdoor patio furniture, a grill, or a refrigerator, thus improving the buyer's ultimate economic deal.

It should also be emphasized that if a buyer or seller has put her best deal on the table, this information should be clearly communicated to the other party. For example, there is nothing wrong in advertising the price for a property as "$300,000 - firm" or to simply state that the seller has the property listed at the bottom price with no flexibility for further reduction. However, even with this type of disclaimer, the seller should not be surprised if a buyer asks for a lower price or other concessions.

Buyers should also communicate to the sellers when an offer is their final offer. Even if the buyer says his final offer is $298,000 many sellers will test the water seeking a higher price by saying that while the parties are close to a deal the best the seller's can offer is $302,500. At this point, the buyer needs to make a choice whether to raise the offer or stand firm.

If the buyer really cannot go higher, it is best to be nice but firm. Say something like, "Please communicate to the sellers that my buyers really love the house. They are not trying to be difficult. However, they simply cannot go above their offer of $298,000. If the seller can meet that price, please let us know. If not, my buyers will be disappointed that they cannot purchase the house but will understand."

If the seller was merely testing the water to see if the buyers would go higher on the price, the above message should close the door on that possibility. If the buyers' offer of $298,000 was acceptable, the seller will likely come back within a few days and agree to accept the buyers' price.

What if the seller really cannot go lower than the $302,500 previously communicated to the buyers? With the buyers having already said their best offer was $298,000 the buyers could lose some credibility if the offer is suddenly increased. At a minimum, they should wait a reasonable period of time before increasing their offer. The buyers are going to lose some face, but offering some rational explanation tends to minimize the damage. For example, the buyers' agent might be able to explain that the buyers were able to get a slightly better rate on their mortgage loan allowing them to make a higher offer. The buyers can possibly say that they received a promise of financial help from a relative allowing for an increased offer. No one likes to deal with a person whom they feel is playing games. Explaining why there has been a major change in position helps a party maintain credibility.

RULE NO. 9   DON'T KNOCK THE HOME YOU'RE
                NEGOTIATING TO BUY

Buyers and their agents must be careful how they raise problems or concerns with a property. While pointing out issues can be helpful in trying to negotiate a better deal, don't go so far that the seller is left wondering why you even want the property, or worse yet, the seller doesn't want you to have the property. Since houses, particularly how they are finished, are a reflection of who a person is, criticizing the house can easily be seen as an attack on the seller.

Our instructions to a buyer viewing a property where the listing agent is going to be present include the directive to not make negative comments about the odor, lack of cleanliness, color, age, type or design of furniture, carpet, walls, tile, etc. It's pretty safe to assume that the seller's bad taste or habits are already well known to the listing agent. Most listing agents will acknowledge the challenges of a property they are trying to sell and without any prompting will usually say something like, "All this house needs..." or "The sale price reflects that the house needs some updating," or "Prior to closing, the seller is going to do the following: _____." Reinforcing the obvious rarely helps the situation. While it is appropriate to raise concerns about a property, the trick is to be positive, objective, and non-judgmental.

Let's look at the following statements a selling agent might make to a listing agent:
- "My buyers really like the house, but value it somewhat differently from the sellers. For the house to meet my buyers' needs they would need to spend about $25,000 right at the time they move in to make certain repairs and to freshen up the house. They are asking the seller to reduce the price to reflect the work."
- "It's not that my buyers think the house is overpriced; they don't. It's simply that they set a limit of $325,000 for their house. The reality is that they have fallen in love with a house that is a little bit out of their reach. If the seller can't meet them at that price they will be disappointed, but they will understand."

- "As you know, my buyers have three children. They love the house, but will need to finish the basement or convert a den into a bedroom. It will cost about $20,000 for this work, and they would like the seller to reduce the price by this amount."
- "The age and condition of the house are actually big pluses for my buyers, because it will give them the opportunity to re-do things to their liking. Now, of course, they do have to figure into their budget the cost of this work...."
- "The seller has done a great job in giving this home a contemporary feel. While we love the home, our tastes are more traditional in nature. As a result we would only be able to buy the house if price concessions were made allowing us to change how the house is finished."

RULE NO. 10   DON'T DRAW LINES IN THE SAND YOU'RE WILLING TO CROSS

There is nothing that will hurt a person's negotiating position more quickly than not doing what you say you are going to do. If you say that an offer is your final offer, it should be your final offer. If you say that an offer is a "take it or leave it" offer, you should be prepared to leave it if it is not taken. If you say that you will go on to a different house if your offer is rejected, go on to a different house.

If you don't do what you say you are going to do, it sends two messages to the other party. The first is that you are not to be trusted. The second is that you want to buy or sell the property more than you've let on. Neither of these messages is appropriate to send to the other party in a negotiation.

We also recommend that you do not make threats often. The nature of a negotiation is give-and-take and compromise. When lines are drawn in the sand, particularly when done too early in the negotiation, it can come across as heavy-handed and offensive. Late in a negotiation, however, line-drawing can help wrap-up a difficult process. Let's say a seller sends to the buyer a powerful message like, "I can't take less than $298,000. Anything less than that and I'll have to bring money to the closing." The buyer is being signaled that the end of the negotiation is near and the seller has reached the end of her rope. The buyer now needs to decide if she is willing to do the deal on or near the terms set forth by the seller.

To recap, the basic DOs of negotiation are to: be observant, be friendly, be curious, be patient, and be reasonable in setting time frames. The basic DON'Ts of negotiation are: don't sweat the small stuff, don't put your commission into play in the negotiation, don't paint yourself into a corner, don't knock the home you're negotiating to buy, and don't draw lines in the sand you're willing to cross. These are all basic, fundamental guidelines that apply to all negotiations. Our next chapter will go beyond the foundations and give you more specific tools to use.

Chapter 10

RULES FOR THE STARTING TEAM

Now we move on to some more specific rules that will help you fine tune your negotiations. You will see in greater detail how elements like your attitude and approach will affect the process, what to watch for in the overall movement of a negotiation, and some tips on using the end of a negotiation to your advantage.

Attitude and Approach

The next five rules we present all affect your own general attitude and approach to a negotiation. As you read each one, think about instances in which your attitude was not as described, and the effect that had on your previous negotiations, or think about an upcoming negotiation, and picture yourself handling it with these attitudes clearly in operation. Use this section as part of your mental preparation and see what a difference it can make.

RULE NO. 11   BE CONFIDENT IN YOURSELF AND IN YOUR COMMUNICATIONS

Regardless of whether an offer is fair, good, or great, it is always important to communicate it with confidence. Lack of confidence can be communicated in many ways. We have participated in numerous negotiations where a party on the other side made a very good offer but later refers to it as an "initial offer." We have also had parties say that if the offer was not acceptable to please submit a counteroffer. Parties may present an offer and say something like, "I don't know what your client will think of this offer, but I thought we'd run it up the flag pole." Finally, we have heard offers prefaced with, "I know this offer is low, but..."

All of these communications include the message that the person making the offer doesn't believe in it and that a much better offer will be forthcoming if the other party asks. An offer presented with confidence is more likely to engender a positive response than one presented with an apology.

It must be remembered that the value of any particular piece of real estate is subject to differing opinions and is best thought of as being in a range of values rather than as a precise number. As a result, many sellers and listing agents will list properties not really knowing what the property will sell for or how long it will take to sell. If a buyer's agent acts like the offer is a good one, it will more likely than not be perceived as such. Why is this the case? It's simple. Let's say a property is listed at $500,000 and an offer is confidently made at $400,000. What will the listing agent make of this offer? The answer is that either the seller's property is overpriced, or the buyer's offer is low. However, sometimes a listing agent will not be 100% sure which one it is. She may think the offer is low, but if no other offers have yet been received the agent may also be wondering if she priced the property too high. It could be that the very next week the seller will receive four full-price offers. But then again, the $400,000 offer may be the best offer the seller ever receives. The point is that there is always some degree of uncertainty in the pricing of a property. Acting confidently in presenting an offer is the currency which helps convince someone of its worthiness.

Now of course, there are limits to this statement. If a buyer makes an offer that can only be described as a sow's ear, it doesn't make sense to try to turn it into a silk purse. Telling a party that you know an offer is great (when in fact it's not) can come across as disingenuous and offend the party receiving the offer. On the theory that most people weren't born yesterday, it's a matter of finding the balance between being confident without appearing ridiculous. Even when the agent doesn't have much to offer, the agent can speak with confidence by saying something like, "I'm really excited that my buyer has decided to make this offer. I wasn't sure she was going to."

With regard to being confident generally, we have found that it takes more than just mentally "psyching" yourself up for the negotiation. We strongly believe that having expertise (or at least being perceived as having expertise) greatly adds to one's confidence as an effective negotiator. Think back to the first time you negotiated against a "famous" real estate agent. Odds are you were a little more tongue-tied, had a few more butterflies in your stomach, or felt a little more intimidated than in other negotiations. With fame often comes the perception of expertise (whether deserved or not). Successful, well-known real estate agents will often use their notoriety as a negotiation tool. It allows them to act with what in basketball is referred to as "swagger." They tend to speak more assertively, act more aggressively, and generally exude an air that they know what they're doing. How does a relatively new real estate agent hold their own in negotiating with such a person?

We have two answers. First, take a deep breath before negotiating with a famous agent and remind yourself (repeatedly, if necessary) that everyone puts on their pants one leg at a time.

Second, remember that you have one advantage over the more experienced agent: time. Odds are that the "famous" agent with whom you are negotiating is not going to have the same amount of time as you to prepare for the negotiation, because being successful almost always means there are huge demands on your time. You must therefore use your time wisely to become better prepared than your counterpart on the specific subjects you know will come up in the negotiation. In other words, if you can't be an expert on everything, just try to be an expert on a few things. Focus on learning everything about the particular house and neighborhood in which it is located to level the playing field with the experienced agent. This concentrated expertise will give you the confidence you need to negotiate against the other agent and likely make her think you are a lot more skilled and experienced than you really are.

RULE NO. 12   REPRESENT THE CLIENT – DON'T
                BECOME THE CLIENT

A real estate agent friend shared the following conversation she had with another agent.

> *"I couldn't believe that agent. I called her and told her I would be presenting an offer on her listing. She asked me what the offer was and I told her . . . Well, the other agent tells me the offer is insulting and she won't even present it to her client. I was so angry, I was just speechless. I have a good mind to report her to the real estate commission."*

Why did the conversation engender so much anger? The other agent violated one of the cardinal rules of negotiation - never forget that your job is to represent the client, not become the client. In this case it really doesn't matter whether the other agent thinks the offer is insulting or not since it isn't her house. The only relevant question is what the seller thinks of the offer. The agent's job is to present the offer no matter what.

It would have been fine for the other agent to have said something like, "While I always present all offers to my client, I'm fairly certain that my client will reject this offer as too low." Similarly, it's okay to say, "If my client asks my opinion of this offer, I'm going to have to tell her that I think your offer is too low." When an agent says, "Your offer is a joke" or "I'm insulted by this offer," the agent is speaking as the client. This leaves the party with whom they are negotiating wondering if this is their own opinion or that of the client.

How agents deal with conflict also varies depending on whether they are representing the client or have become the client. Remembering that an agent's role is advisory in nature helps the agent to be more detached and objective in analyzing the negotiation and giving advice as to how best to proceed. There is nothing personal about the conflicts which inevitably occur in any negotiation. Dealing with them is just a normal part of the agent's job. When the agent gets too emotionally involved in the negotiation she becomes subject to the same emotional upheavals that most clients feel in buying or selling property. Conflicts become more personal in nature, objectivity is lost, and in many cases the result is "the blind leading the blind" in navigating the rough waters of negotiation.

RULE NO. 13   REMEMBER – YOU MAY NEED A
                FAVOR FROM THE OTHER SIDE
                BEFORE THE DEAL IS DONE

We have participated in negotiations where parties reached an agreement but then refused to extend even the slightest courtesy to the other party when they sought to renegotiate a minor change to the contract. This "scorched earth" approach will minimize the ability to re-negotiate any detail later, if and when the obstinate party needs a favor themselves.

Sometimes this is a way for one party or the other to make it clear that they hold the high cards in the negotiation, and know it. In a hot condominium conversion market in Florida we've seen owners of apartment complexes use the approach effectively. Oftentimes they would announce they were entertaining bids to buy their property if they were received by a certain date, knowing that there would be several. When soliciting bids they would often set extremely short dates for closing and require non-refundable earnest money payments in the millions of dollars before the buyer even had an opportunity to inspect the property. While such terms would be unheard of in a normal market, apartment owners found condominium converters lined up at their door even when they imposed the most unreasonable requirements. Unwillingness by the seller to give the buyer even the smallest break was a very calculated means of communicating that the seller was going to dictate and control every aspect of the deal.

In other cases, not doing favors is a way of discouraging a party from continually seeking to modify the terms of the sale contract. This recently happened to a buyer client of ours in purchasing a $50 million building. The buyer was marginally qualified to acquire the property and almost immediately after getting the property under contract began to request that the seller relax various provisions in the contract. After this happened the second time the seller's counsel wrote a firm letter to buyer's counsel announcing that no further changes to the contract would be considered, and that the buyer could either close on the property or default on its obligations. The buyer stopped asking for further concessions.

Unlike the lopsided negotiations described above, in most real estate negotiations the parties are more or less equally motivated to consummate the transaction. As such, the parties are more than willing to do the other party small favors and expect the same in return. Clients who take the position that they don't need to help the other party in a negotiation should be reminded that payback can be hell when the shoe is on the other foot.

The adage that what goes around comes around holds true in negotiations. If one party is being difficult, eventually someone will be difficult to her. Our approach to small favors is to bend over backward to do them when requested, particularly if they don't cost the client. Of course, the party being asked for a favor should always consider whether she needs anything in return. There is never anything inappropriate about suggesting a quid pro quo where one favor is exchanged for another.

If the party granting the favor doesn't need one in return we recommend that she still remind the requesting party that she didn't have to do the favor and expects the courtesy to be returned if needed later. While this creates no legal obligation, it puts the favor-granting party in a position to assume the high ground and express indignation should a later request for a return favor be denied.

RULE NO. 14   BE RESPONSIVE TO THE OTHER SIDE

Sellers will often not respond to a low offer. The famous newspaper magnate, William Randolph Hearst, regularly followed this approach and the quote "Silence answers itself" is attributed to him. Nevertheless, silence in the face of an offer is not a good way to encourage further negotiation. Instead, it usually makes the person who made the low offer angry. (This is very different from the silence that is sometimes truly golden that we mentioned earlier when discussing brief periods of silence during a face-to-face conversation.) While not all offers need to be countered, parties negotiating in good faith should at least respond.

We strongly encourage the listing agent to at least call the selling agent to say that although the offer had been received, there will not be a counteroffer as the initial offer was too low. While the likelihood that a buyer who initially makes a low offer will end up buying the property at a respectable price is remote, stranger things have happened. Occasionally there is some misunderstanding on the part of a buyer who makes an offer that is not worthy of a counter. We have seen such instances in which buyers were mistakenly told by a "friend of a friend" that a house could be purchased for "a song." Similarly, a buyer may make a very low offer just to see the seller's reaction.

If the seller maintains open communication there is an opportunity for negotiations to continue.

RULE NO. 15   ENLIST THE OTHER AGENT'S HELP

In every negotiation you will run into obstacles. Perhaps the parties are not able to agree on a major issue and there doesn't seem to be any way to break the impasse. Let's look at the following scenario and see how you can turn your challenges into those of the other party.

You are representing a buyer who has made several offers to purchase a property originally listed at $700,000 but more realistically worth around $650,000. The seller has come down to $685,000 but won't go lower. The price is high relative to other properties which have recently sold in the neighborhood. The house needs to be painted, the roof replaced, and the kitchen updated. But the buyer also wants an older craftsman style home and this particular house is one of the few in the neighborhood, so the seller feels justified in holding the line on her price. The buyer's agent might decide to share with the listing agent her view that the seller is being unreasonable by refusing to lower her price.

Although this may make the buyer's agent momentarily feel better, it doesn't do anything to advance the negotiation. Most listing agents will simply shrug at such a comment. Here's what the buyer's agent might say to obtain the listing agent's support in convincing the seller to reduce the price.

Buyer's Agent: "You know, I'm trying to figure out if we can close the gap between our clients on the price of the property. My client wants the house, but here's the problem. Except for newly constructed homes, your client's property is about $30,000 higher than others on the market. Here's a copy of what I gave my client so you can see for yourself. My client has had a contractor look at the items needing immediate replacement and it totals about $15,000. My client really likes the house but unless I can show her something to support a higher price no deal is going to be made here. Anything you can do to help me would be greatly appreciated."

Now if you think about the above scenario, the agent, without being argumentative, was able to rationally communicate why she thought the price of the property was too high. Rather than disagreeing with the listing agent, the buyer's agent is enlisting her help to get the seller to lower the price. If the listing agent is inexperienced and unaware of the true value of the property, giving her the information about the value of the property may help when she goes to talk to the seller. Conversely, the listing agent may provide the buyer's agent information about the property which helps her to justify a higher price to the buyer. Either way, the exchange of information between the parties should increase the likelihood of a successful outcome to the negotiation.

Overall Movement of a Negotiation

The next three rules all address how a negotiation flows. There is of course a give-and-take to any negotiation. How do you know when you can "give" and when you need to "take"? Keep these three rules in mind, and this will be an easier question to answer when you are in the middle of any negotiation.

RULE NO. 16   DON'T BID AGAINST YOURSELF
Imagine you are working with a client who becomes interested in buying some land that is not yet listed for sale. You approach the owner and ask her if she would consider selling. The seller says "yes." When you ask the seller for a price, she tells you she's not sure and to make her an offer. If you are the seller this isn't a bad strategy. Had you stated a price it might have been lower than what the buyer was willing to offer. By inviting an offer the seller can make sure she is leaving no money on the table.

In most negotiations it is the party who wants something the most who makes the first offer. Usually that party is the seller when she lists a property for sale at a certain price. In the example discussed above the typical situation was reversed because the buyer was the one who approached the seller seeking to buy the land. The buyer has little choice but to make the first offer in this situation.

Let's say, however, that the buyer offers $800,000 for the property and the seller responds by saying, "That's not enough. You need to make a better offer." If the buyer continues to make offers without any counteroffer from the seller, the negotiation is completely one-sided. The buyer's offers are just going up while the seller is not making a counteroffer.

It was reasonable in this situation for the buyer to have made the first offer. However, once the seller said that the offer wasn't good enough the buyer should have taken a different approach. It would have been more appropriate for the buyer to say, "You obviously have a price in mind. Tell me the price you're hoping for so we don't waste time." If the seller states a price, the negotiation has begun. Notice that we intentionally used the phrase "the price you're hoping for" in order to leave the door open for further negotiations. This is much more effective than asking for the other party's bottom line. If the seller is unwilling to state a price, the buyer must decide how much she really wants the property. Good preparation (before making the offer) will help the buyer determine how comfortable she is in making another, and how high she is willing to go. (See Part II regarding behind-the-scenes preparation.) While the buyer may make one more offer, most will cut off the negotiation and tell the seller to call him or her when the seller has set a price.

There are also subtle ways to encourage a party to negotiate against themselves. One way to do so when a low offer is made is to say something like the following:

> *"I've reviewed your clients' offer and while I certainly want to get this property sold, I'm frankly concerned that their offer will cause my client to react negatively. I'll present the offer if you want, but I'd urge you to take the offer back to your clients and review with them whether this is really the offer your clients want to make."*

This approach can be a bit disarming to the agent making the offer. While you're telling her that her clients' offer stinks, you're just doing it in a way which makes it look like you are on her side and trying to help her. Of course, agents using this strategy should make sure that they do not run afoul of their general duty to timely present all offers.

RULE NO. 17   BE WARY OF A "LET'S SPLIT THE DIFFERENCE" STRATEGY

One of the more common negotiating strategies is to offer to split the difference between your position and that of the other party to the negotiation in order to bring a negotiation to a successful conclusion. This allows the party suggesting it to at least appear to be taking the high road by offering to meet the other party halfway.

Splitting the difference is logical when the parties are close in price and the midway point is reasonably related to the true value of the property. It does not make sense when the parties are further apart on price and the mid-way point is not reasonably related to the true value of the property. Let's say a buyer and a seller are $100,000 apart on the price of a particular property. The seller who was at $500,000 has been reducing the price in increments of $5,000. The buyer has generally been increasing the price in increments of $10,000. If the parties are $100,000 apart, it makes great sense for the buyer to offer to split the difference on the sale price of the property at $450,000. The same cannot be said for the seller. Here's why.

Since the buyer was increasing offers at roughly twice the rate as the seller was decreasing counteroffers, had the negotiations continued, the property would have sold for a little less than $470,000. Splitting the difference would have caused the seller to get less money than if the negotiations continued on the original path.

The real problem with splitting the difference is that it is an arbitrary approach and does not necessarily have any bearing on the true value of a property. If the buyer's offers were low and the seller's counteroffers were fair relative to the true value of the property, splitting the difference hurts the seller. The same is true in reverse.

Let's say that a property has been independently appraised by two different appraisers as having a value of $600,000. The market is generally good and the seller hopes to get close to her listing price. A buyer makes a low offer of $500,000. The seller counters at $595,000. The buyer at this point offers to split the difference between the two prices at $547,500. This may sound fair in that it is halfway between the buyer's last offer and the seller's counteroffer. However, if the property is worth $600,000 and the market is good, accepting $547,500 may be more of a price reduction for the property than the seller needs to make. In this case arbitrarily splitting the difference may not be a smart move. Before accepting a "let's split the difference" approach, the seller should always consider the importance to her of getting her target price, and think about how splitting the difference helps her to achieve that goal.

When an offer is made to split the difference both sides need to: (1) carefully look at the numbers, and (2) ask themselves whether splitting the difference is merely pulling a number out of the air or whether it relates to something logical relative to the property.

RULE NO. 18   GO BACKWARD OR FORWARD TO GET A NEGOTIATION DONE

We have seen many negotiations where one of the parties decides she doesn't like the deal she is about to strike and reverses direction in the negotiation. Usually this comes about as a result of not knowing the true value of what is being sold. For example, a seller may tentatively agree to sell a property for $350,000 and be in negotiations over repairs when the seller discovers the true value of the property is $425,000.

At this point the seller reverses positions and revises the price upward. What should the buyer do in such a situation? The answer depends on how good a deal the buyer was getting. If the property is still a bargain, we would encourage buyers to swallow their pride and buy the property. This is because the negotiation should not be about ego or one-upsmanship, but about reaching a mutually agreeable deal. Prideful buyers will sometimes walk away from these types of negotiations and lose out on a great deal. There is an important lesson to be learned from such a loss. When you can get a great deal, don't delay or become greedy. Close the deal quickly and enjoy your good fortune!

Whether buyers or sellers are willing to go backward in a negotiation should largely be a function of why they are being asked to do so. If the request has come about because new information is learned about a property's value, the parties should expect some price adjustment up or down. If the request is coming about because of a perception that the relative negotiating positions of the parties has changed, we would resist going along with the request. The concern with going backward in this situation is that once you start down this slippery slope there may be no end to going further and further backward.

If you must go backward, it is always advisable to do it as part of bringing the negotiation to a close. So, for example, a buyer in response to being asked to go backward on price might say something like the following:

"Look, it's my policy never to go backward in a negotiation. While I might consider doing so this one time, send me a signed contract with all of the other changes we discussed and I'll decide."

Using the End of a Negotiation to Advantage

Expert negotiators will use the entire process - even the end - to help their client come out a winner. Here are a few tips to help you make the most of the end of a negotiation process.

RULE NO. 19   USE DUE DILIGENCE PERIODS TO
GET A SECOND BITE AT THE APPLE

In commercial real estate transactions there is a practice known as "re-trading the deal." It works something like this. A buyer will get a property under contract by outbidding other buyers. During the due diligence period that follows (when the buyer can still get out of the deal), the buyer then consciously looks for issues to raise to seek a reduction in the price. The square footage of the property may be less than represented. Defects in the property are discovered which are expensive to fix. The property may need to be retrofitted to comply with federal laws or to remove some dangerous product. These "discoveries" are communicated by the buyer as if she has never been in this situation before. The buyer informs the seller that while she wants the property, she will have to reluctantly terminate the contract unless a significant price concession is made. The seller at this point has to either agree to the reduction or start the process all over again with another buyer, who may or may not appear just over the horizon.

Many residential real estate sales contracts also give the buyer the right to ask for repairs after entering into the contract. If the seller does not agree to the requested repairs the buyer can terminate the contract. Other contracts give buyers the right to terminate a contract for any reason within a specified number of days after the contract has been signed. These provisions are designed to protect buyers in the event they discover major problems with the property during what are known as due diligence or inspection periods. These inspection periods can also be used by buyers to negotiate further repair concessions. Buyers have two advantages in these situations. First, once most sellers enter into a real estate sales contract they begin to think of their homes as being sold and start to focus on moving. Psychologically they have become more invested in the idea that the property is going to be sold and to this particular buyer. As a result, sellers are usually willing to make more concessions than they might with a buyer with whom they have not yet entered into a contract. The more time that passes, the more a seller may feel the buyer has them over a barrel with regard to a requested repair. If the choice is to agree to make the repair or risk losing the deal, many sellers will agree, however reluctantly, to make the repair rather than having to start the sale process all over again with another buyer. Second, if an inspector discovers legitimate latent defects with a property most sellers are willing to accept responsibility for repair. Most sellers understand that since the price of the property was negotiated without knowledge of the defect, its discovery must lead to the seller either agreeing to the repair or making some adjustment in the price. The buyer in these situations is using time to her advantage. The more time the buyer is given to get out of a contract, the more leverage the buyer has to demand concessions.

How can the seller's exposure in these negotiations be limited? There are several options. First, the listing agent can advise the seller to leave room for further concessions during a due diligence period. Second, the listing agent may also want to advise the seller to have an inspection done of their property prior to listing it for sale. This tends to minimize the potential for surprises. The seller knows in advance what repairs may be needed, and can either choose to make the repairs in advance, or make an informed choice about how much "wiggle room" they want to allow in the negotiations to cover any requested repairs. Third, the listing agent can do more to clarify to buyers that the sale price of the property reflects those defects disclosed by the seller. Encourage your seller clients to include this caveat in their property disclosure statement and in the sale contract itself. While this will obviously not guarantee that a buyer will not ask for further concessions, it at least gives the seller a legitimate basis to reject such a request. Fourth, the seller can try to limit the duration of a due diligence period. If the seller then has to put the property back on the market because the buyer and seller could not agree on the repairs to be made to the property, the seller will not feel that she has lost a significant amount of time with the first buyer.

Sellers can also protect themselves by insisting that the property be sold "as is" or by including a special stipulation in the contract providing that the buyer agrees to accept any defects disclosed in writing by the seller prior to entering into the contract, and will not request the repair of any disclosed defect. This type of provision is known as a "partial as-is" clause. With such a special stipulation, the buyer can normally request the repair of any later-discovered defects not disclosed by the seller.

Finally, sellers have to be comfortable telling buyers no when they are unwilling to make further concessions. Otherwise a buyer may continue pushing for more. Chances for a successful negotiation increase when the listing agent helps the seller to have realistic expectations. Additionally, a good listing agent will signal the buyer's agent when the end of concessions is either near or has arrived.

RULE NO. 20   ACCEPT THAT SOME DEALS JUST
                WEREN'T MEANT TO HAPPEN

How can this be a part of using the end of a negotiation to your advantage? Simple. It can help you and your client maintain a fresh outlook and not get bogged down in an impossible situation. Think of it as a way to avoid a quicksand type of negotiation - you know, the type that appears to be on solid ground, but in reality is a bog that will keep pulling you down the more you struggle to free yourself. If you (and your client) are willing to accept that some deals just weren't meant to happen, you avoid the sense of "losing" something you "should" have won, and are free to approach your next negotiation with a winning perspective. Let's look at a specific example of what we mean.

One of the authors tried to buy undeveloped land that was worth an estimated $100,000. It was a large piece of property that abutted a stream. The stream setback requirements in the local zoning ordinance effectively allowed only 5% of the land to be developed. The author wanted to buy the property because it was next to some other property he already owned and would allow him to develop the overall site at a greater density.

The owner's real estate agent said that his client wouldn't take less than $325,000 for the land. The author had several long telephone conversations and a meeting with the owner's agent where he tried to educate him as to the true value of the property. While the agent heard what the author was saying, in the end his client wouldn't budge from his price.

The author offered a bit more than $100,000 for the property and the offer was rejected without a counteroffer. What happened next? The author told the agent that if the seller ever reconsidered and was willing to sell the property for what had been offered to please call. He then moved on and didn't give the property another thought. Some deals just aren't meant to be.

Not all buyers and sellers have realistic expectations. (Maybe it was the author who had the unrealistic expectations.) No two pieces of real estate are quite the same and, in the end, it's what a willing buyer and seller agree upon that determines the deal. It is futile to actively pursue a deal when the parties are so far apart in how they value a property. In such cases the only rational strategy is to move on. In the above situation the seller may or may not come back at a lower price in the future.

The same philosophy applies equally to both the buying and selling of homes, not just undeveloped land. A good negotiator educates the client on the reality that there are other houses that meet the buyer's needs. A buyer can make an informed decision to either walk away from a great house that can't be had for a reasonable price, or to accept paying a higher price.

In our next chapter we'll discuss some additional tools that will help in more difficult negotiations.

Chapter 11

RULES FOR ALL-STARS

Our final guidelines for you are good to remember whenever you're involved in a particularly difficult negotiation, or you suspect that one may develop that way. The difficulty may be a client's strong personality, or the complexity of a deal with some inherently sticky issues, or a situation where one party is asking for the moon and the other is only offering them a telescope aimed in that particular direction. The rules we discuss in this chapter will help you with these circumstances. We've broken them down into three categories: characters (yours, mine and ours), the angels in the details, and communicating the right message.

Characters - Yours, Mine and Ours

RULE NO. 21   GUARD YOUR GOOD CHARACTER –
IT'S YOUR SECRET WEAPON

As a young Atlanta lawyer, one of the authors (who we'll refer to as Mr. X) had several cases against a much older attorney whose first name was Clifford. Clifford was the consummate southern gentleman. He was always complimentary of Mr. X in front of his client, always did what he said he was going to do, was always polite, and went out of his way to be helpful. If Mr. X needed a survey or a copy of the zoning conditions in a case, Clifford would have them hand delivered to Mr. X within an hour after he and Mr. X spoke. All of this was at the same time Clifford and Mr. X were representing their respective clients in some lively real estate disputes.

Watching Clifford taught the author a lot about how to earn the respect of colleagues and about how to negotiate, and helped him realize there is nothing personal about the different positions being advanced in a negotiation. It is business; but you can still be friendly and professional. The author also realized that it was much easier to negotiate a settlement when Clifford was on the other side. When negotiating with Clifford and a question would arise about his client's motivation or intent, Mr. X believed Clifford because he had proven himself to be trustworthy.

While there are many benefits to getting involved in a Board of REALTORS,® one benefit that is not emphasized enough is that it gives agents a chance to network with other agents and build friendships, rapport, and trust. Building positive rapport with other agents makes life easier and increases the likelihood of a successful negotiation. Think how you feel when the agent on the other side of a real estate transaction is someone that you know, like, and trust. Now think how you feel when the agent with whom you are negotiating is someone that you do not know, or whom you do not like or trust. All other things being equal, with which agent are you likely to have the greatest success in negotiating the purchase or sale of a home?

While a few agents might argue that they will do the same job negotiating for their clients regardless of the personality and character of the agent on the other side, most will acknowledge that, human nature being what it is, their feelings and level of trust for the other agent will affect the negotiation's outcome.

To a large degree your level of trust of another agent influences whether you give them the benefit of the doubt when a problem arises. For example, an agent prepares a "clean" or conformed copy of a contract and omits a key special stipulation. If the agent is someone you know and trust, you accept that it was a mistake or oversight on the agent's part. The opposite conclusion may be reached if you are dealing with an agent you don't trust, or with whom you've had previous bad experiences. If you guard your own reputation as an agent of good character, negotiations will more often result in a deal being reached.

RULE NO. 22   WHEN YOUR CLIENT IS A
               "CHARACTER," CONSIDER LEAVING
               THE WIZARD OF OZ BEHIND
               THE CURTAIN

In real estate transactions brokers are ethically, and in many cases legally, prevented from negotiating directly with another broker's client when the broker has an exclusive agency or an exclusive right to sell with the client. It is typical for both clients to remain unknown. Good negotiators can use this to their advantage.

By not directly involving the client in the negotiation, the negotiator can impart to the other side exaggerated qualities and traits of the client. Lawyers use this tactic all the time. For example, a client receives a demand letter with a threat of a law suit. In such cases their lawyer's job is to evaluate the strength of the threat and the potential that the opposition will take the dispute to the next level and actually file suit. If the party threatening suit is personally friendly, mild-mannered, or generally rational, their lawyer will likely keep him or her away from the defendant's lawyer. People with these traits are usually perceived as being less likely to file lawsuits and may be more open to settling a dispute for a smaller amount. It's helpful in such circumstances to keep the client in the background in order to pursue a larger settlement.

As a young attorney representing condominium associations against developers in construction defects litigation, one of the authors was able to successfully use this technique. Most of the developers feared the so-called "condo commandos" running these associations. Rather than dispelling these fears (which were normally unfounded), it was to our advantage to accentuate the "boogey-man" qualities of the client. The author always discussed this approach with the client first. Clients quickly understand that developers may be willing to settle even marginal claims if they believe their opponent is angry enough to file suit to obtain a satisfactory resolution of the claim.

This same principle has application in real estate negotiations where the buyer and seller are represented by their respective agents. Sometimes buyers and sellers are such difficult personalities that it is easier to keep them in the background where their negative qualities can be softened. At other times there may be value in describing a client as increasingly irritated or offended (when they may not be) as a means of ending negotiations.

The exaggerated use of this technique entails risks. It can raise ethical issues with regard to the honest representation of clients and fair negotiations with the other agent and clients. For example, what if an agent states that a client is "strongly offended" when in fact they might only be moderately annoyed? We do not think there is an ethical problem with an agent saying this as a negotiation ploy, so long as the client consents to the approach and accepts the downside risk if it backfires.

From our vantage point, the job of any good negotiator is to try to achieve the client's goals using negotiating tactics and strategies which the client is aware of and approves. Let's say a client thinks you are going to use a risk-averse strategy to try to buy a property, but the agent instead has a high-risk strategy. The agent may get the property for the buyer at a lower price. However, if the agent loses the deal the agent has certainly not done the client any favors and, if her actions are ever discovered, she may be sued.

As lawyers we will not intentionally keep a client in the background when they have a particularly difficult personality without first explaining why. We have even counseled such clients, "Joe, let me finish this negotiation. You're a great guy, but with your strong personality I may be the better one to deal with these last couple of issues." While a client may occasionally override the recommendation, most strong personalities will go along with this so long as it is part of a planned strategy.

RULE NO. 23   ADD A NEW CHARACTER TO SALVAGE A FAILING NEGOTIATION

Sometimes a negotiation will hit a wall where neither side will budge and the deal appears dead, or at least terminally ill. While some deals are worth letting die there are others which, objectively, should come together. Sometimes the clients or their agents have a personality conflict that interferes with their ability to reach an agreement. In other cases there is some breach of trust (real or perceived) which makes it impossible for the parties to have further productive discussions.

When this happens to one of our clients we may call the attorney representing the other party and say the following:

"You know, sometimes when their respective clients have gotten cross with one another it's the job of good lawyers to put their heads together and try to come up with a deal that at least the lawyers believe makes sense. I think this is one of those situations."

Without making any promises, the lawyers then go to their respective clients and try to talk to them. Agents can handle negotiations between clients the same way. The agents can negotiate the issues between themselves without the involvement of their clients. Once they determine what they believe is fair they return to their clients to try to get them on board.

In other cases, the dispute will be between the agents. When agents see this occurring they should give serious consideration to introducing someone new to the negotiation to represent that client and overcome the obstacle. With so many agents working together in teams, one way to do this is to shift the responsibility for negotiating a deal to another member of the team. In other cases a good agent may ask her broker to call the broker for the other party to see if the issues can be resolved at that level.

When things are going well in a negotiation there should not be an effort to fix what isn't broken. However, if the deal looks like it's failing there is little to lose by bringing in a pinch-hitter who may have better success at satisfactorily concluding a negotiation. You will obviously want to make such a change only if the client agrees to it in advance.

The Angels in the Details

You've probably heard the phrase "the devil is in the details." We prefer to switch that around a bit and focus on the more creative, positive ways you can handle some details. These "angels" will strengthen your negotiation rather than tear it apart. Consider situations in which the following three rules might come into play.

RULE NO. 24   DEFER TOUGH ISSUES FOR THE END OF A LENGTHY NEGOTIATION

When there are many issues to be negotiated one classic strategy is for agents to encourage clients to set aside the hardest issues for later. This does two positive things. First, it builds momentum in the negotiation. There's nothing better than getting parties to agree early on issues and make them feel as though they can overcome the remaining differences. Second, the more time is invested in a negotiation the harder it is for either party to walk away from it. As the issues start to narrow the agents should encourage their clients to be thinking about the remaining issues and how they can be resolved.

If the deferred issue is an economic one (such as a difference in price), offering to split the difference is usually the first solution. (See our discussion of this approach in Rule No. 16.) But sometimes there are other "deal-killer" issues for one party or the other that remain to be negotiated. For example, buyers with children may be unwilling to purchase a property unless the closing is before the start of the school year. The seller, perhaps for business reasons, may be equally adamant about not wanting to move until three weeks after school starts. One obvious compromise is to close midway between the dates desired by each party. Another approach is to discover if either client has another "hot button" to be used as a concession for compromising on the closing date.

It should also be remembered that in the end most issues can be reduced to economic terms. In a dispute over a move-in date the cost of storing furniture or of a hotel room may ultimately be the currency needed to resolve the problem.

RULE NO. 25   PACKAGING COUNTS

While this may sound silly, how an offer is packaged can sometimes make a difference in whether or not it is accepted. By this we mean both the terms of the offer itself, and how it is then presented. Agents put together offers as a "package" comprised of features such as price, included appliances, or payment of closing costs. The more subtle part of packaging involves presentation of the offer. For example, let's say a buyer offers $810,000 on a sale price of $900,000. Most successful agents will make sure the offer is presented or packaged as 90% of the sale price because this sounds much better than an offer which is $90,000 less than the seller's asking price.

Another aspect of packaging is reworking the offer to address concerns articulated by the other party. Some sellers may be particularly sensitive about paying for a particular item, such as making any contribution toward closing costs. Agents should be on the lookout for resistance to paying certain costs. If a seller keeps rejecting a request to pay closing costs, for example, it may be a good idea to compensate by modifying other financial pieces of an offer rather than continuing to push an item for which no concession is likely to be made. Before doing this, however, you should ask the agent on the other side if your perception of resistance is correct and, if so, why there is such resistance.

In repackaging an offer, be careful not to insult the other party. Making the same financial offer but merely expressing it in different terms can hurt the negotiation.

There is also a risk in constantly repackaging an offer. The party on the other side may become confused or think that you or your client are trying to trick her. A repackaged offer should be a better offer than the one it followed. In a real estate deal the idea of repackaging is to try to tweak an offer to put it in terms most likely to be favorably received by the other party.

RULE NO. 26 THE NUMBERS GAME –
PROGRESSIVELY MOVE AWAY FROM
ROUND NUMBERS, OR CONSIDER
BRACKETING TO CLOSE A LARGE GAP

In real estate negotiations, offers and counteroffers are usually made in round numbers to the nearest hundred or thousand dollars. This makes sense when there is a large difference between what the buyer is willing to pay and what the seller is willing to accept. As the parties start to get closer to their target prices, we often recommend they consider making an offer in a very specific dollar amount that at least creates an impression of a great deal of thought.

Let's say that a seller, after a series of offers and counteroffers, comes back with a counteroffer of $303,285. This amount is so specific it doesn't appear to have been pulled out of a hat (although it may have been). Instead it helps to create an impression that the seller has struggled to come up with the offer and that the amount is related to a particular amount the seller must clear from the transaction.

Going from an offer rounded to the nearest thousand to an offer rounded to the nearest ten dollars also signals that the seller is coming to the end of the negotiation and that the increments for further offers and counteroffers will generally be smaller.

Bracketing is a technique sometimes used by lawyers in mediations when the parties are quite far apart. This involves both parties making simultaneous large moves towards each other to try and narrow the gap. Let's say the seller is demanding $450,000 and the buyer is offering $50,000. The parties are making progress, but in very small increments. After three or four rounds they have only moved to $435,000 for the seller and $75,000 for the buyer. At this point it becomes clear that either (1) both parties have expectations that are nowhere close to each other or (2) each side is still posturing and no one wants to be the first to make a significant move.

In order to get the parties closer together the buyer might suggest that she will increase her offer from $75,000 to $150,000 if the seller agrees to simultaneously reduce her demand from $435,000 to $300,000. This offer does not immediately result in a settlement, but it narrows the space between each sides' position and gets the parties closer together. It can also be a way for one party, the buyer in this example, to try to get the seller to come down on the price in greater increments. Note that in this example the buyer's offer only increased by $75,000 while the seller's demand would come down by $135,000.

Communicating the Right Message

Our final four rules for this chapter focus on communicating. The first deals with the method of communication, the second with how to convey an attitude of urgency, the third and fourth with conveying your attitude about the close of a negotiation (regardless of whether it results in a sale or not).

RULE NO. 27   FACE-TO-FACE COMMUNICATION
                TRUMPS E-MAIL AND THE
                TELEPHONE

One of the things we have noticed over the years is that people tend to be less rude in person than they are over the phone or in a letter, facsimile, or e-mail. This observation has obvious implications for negotiation. When you reach a delicate point it is best to deal with it in person. The problem with this is that in most real estate transactions today, little is done in person. Perhaps this should change. We suspect that more deals would come together if agents took more time to get to know one another and to extend themselves to other agents. Delivering a contract in person or meeting an agent at a coffee shop to review some unique aspect of a deal might achieve far better results than sending it by facsimile or e-mail. In any negotiation there are times when there is some type of miscommunication, misunderstanding, or a potential break-down of trust that could threaten to unravel a transaction. This is less likely to happen if the deal is explained face-to-face. An ounce of prevention is worth a pound of cure.

RULE NO. 28   LEARN TO CREATE A SENSE OF URGENCY

When does a negotiation reach the point at which patience is less than a virtue? When action becomes a necessity. It could be the action required to get a negotiation off the ground, or to break an impasse during a negotiation, or to wrap up a drawn out negotiation process. You will at times need to create a sufficient sense of urgency to cause one of the parties to act. There are subtle – and not so subtle – ways to create urgency. Circumstances will obviously dictate which approach makes the most sense.

One example would be the very tentative buyer. Let's assume that a husband and wife have looked at a house on three different occasions and have said that they love the house, yet they have not made an offer. Many agents in this position (whether representing seller or buyer) will try to determine what obstacles exist to making an offer and try to eliminate them. This approach is very rational and works well in many negotiations. But there are other ways to motivate leisurely buyers to take action.

Let's look at a few statements to see how they contribute to a sense of urgency.

- If you like the house at all, you should know that I'm showing it to a couple later this week for the third time. They're bringing the husband's parents with them to get their opinion on the house.
- By the way, a renovator is looking at the house pretty seriously. He's running numbers to see if it makes sense to fix it up for resale.
- These are the last units left in this phase. Once these units are sold, the developer will be opening a new phase of the condominium with a significant price hike.

SECRETS OF WINNING THE REAL ESTATE NEGOTIATION GAME©

- There's only one other property on the lake for sale right now, but it barely has a view of the water. If you want to live on Smith Lake and have this type of view, this home is pretty much your only option.
- While my client appreciates your offer, it is not in the ball park of what my client can accept. We hope you will quickly consider making a much higher offer. Please remember that my seller only needs one serious buyer to get her house sold. With the amount of traffic going through the house, that buyer could come along at any time.

All of these statements are designed to get the buyers thinking that they had better move quickly, but not by taking a high-pressure approach. The agent is merely sharing information that most buyers would want to know.

When a listing agent is thinking about how to create a sense of urgency to motivate a prospective buyer to action, she should focus on what is distinct or special about a property that would cause it to be sold quickly to that particular buyer. The agent must know not only the property, but also the buyer. A house with a very expensive swimming pool may be special – except to a buyer with a terrible fear of the water. Be creative. Think of more than one special feature of any property you have listed that will help to create that sense of urgency when needed. If there is nothing particularly outstanding about the property, encourage the seller to list it at a great price so that price alone makes the property stand out.

Patience can also be less than a virtue when a negotiation has reached an impasse. Suppose the buyers in the example above have finally made an offer, the seller has countered, and negotiations have progressed very slowly. You have now seemingly hit a dead-end, and are seeing no movement from these same buyers. As listing agent you may try a less subtle reminder to break through the barrier:

> *I just want to remind you that until we have a fully inked deal, we will continue to market the property to other prospective buyers.*

This more direct approach can be used by both buyers and sellers alike. For example, a buyer looking to break an impasse might make the following statements:

- It would be a shame if the deal is allowed to fall apart over _____. It may be awhile before another buyer comes along who is willing to pay this much for the property.
- You should be aware that my client's patience is wearing thin. While I don't know whether she will pull the plug on the deal, I've seen her do so in similar situations.

Rarely, a not-so-subtle approach must be taken which usually involves giving the other party a deadline or an ultimatum:

- You have until 5:00 p.m. to accept our counteroffer. If you have not done so, my client is moving on to another property.
- This offer is the best we can do. You should know that we have another buyer interested in the property. If you don't accept by the end of the weekend, we will be forced to begin negotiations with her.

When you find yourself in one of these "stalemate" situations, remember that subtle ways of creating urgency are generally preferable to giving a party an ultimatum. The all-or-nothing nature of an ultimatum affects both parties. If an ultimatum is given and ignored, the party giving it has little choice but to make good on her threat and to walk away from the table. Subtle forms of instilling urgency give the negotiator more wiggle room. If the negotiator is unsuccessful in creating sufficient urgency to move things along, the negotiation normally continues and the parties simply modify their strategy.

RULE NO. 29   LET THE OTHER SIDE KNOW YOU ARE
                        WILLING TO WALK AWAY
While it's a high-risk strategy, being able to walk away from a deal is sometimes a good way to help make the deal come together.

A good friend of ours, Mary Lou, has great success with this approach. Recently Mary Lou and several other agents were competing for a plum $4.2 million listing. All of the agents were interviewed by the sellers. Mary Lou knew she was the last agent to be interviewed that day. When she walked into the seller's living room, Mr. Seller said something like the following:

> *"I just want you to know that we've already interviewed four other agents. While I want to hear your ideas on marketing our home, you should know that the other agents are all willing to discount their commissions pretty significantly. You need to address the commission issue in your presentation because if you don't agree to a large reduction, you won't be considered for the job."*

At this point Mary Lou started gathering her things and politely said it had been nice to meet the seller and that she was sorry they wouldn't be working together. Mr. Seller immediately asked where Mary Lou was going. She quietly explained that since she didn't cut her commission on any transaction she did not want to waste the seller's time by making a presentation.

Mr. Seller, looking very surprised, commented that if her marketing strategy justified a full commission he was willing to pay it. Needless to say, Mary Lou ended up with the listing and at a full commission. The seller, a chief executive officer of a publicly-traded company, would later report that he was floored by the gumption displayed by Mary Lou and that alone made her a very attractive candidate.

Now it should be noted that not everyone can pull off what Mary Lou was able to achieve. The fact that Mary Lou was a well-known and successful agent gave her a leg up in employing this high-stakes approach. She was also armed with a pretty good marketing plan.

RULE NO. 30   THANK THE OTHER SIDE FOR THEIR PARTICIPATION – EVEN IF NO DEAL IS REACHED

We end this chapter with a variation on our first rule - being friendly. When was the last time anyone thanked you for a failed negotiation? Usually if a deal goes south, so does everyone's attitude. However, no harm can come from telling the other agent that you enjoyed working with her and that while this deal did not result in a sale, you appreciate her time and effort and look forward to working with her in the future. It will help you in future dealings with her and may just be the edge you need when the next deal with that agent comes along.

Our next chapter discusses some styles or "postures" of negotiators you may encounter, and will from time to time find useful to employ yourself.

Chapter 12

IDENTIFYING DIFFERENT PLAYING STRATEGIES

Being attuned to different negotiating postures or approaches is one of the best ways to learn how to become a great negotiator. Recognizing how the other party is approaching the negotiations gives you insight on how to respond appropriately. Negotiations always involve some degree of psychology. Like breaking a code, recognizing a negotiating posture minimizes its psychological impact and a good negotiator can often turn that to her advantage. Let's look at examples of common negotiation strategies and styles to see if you recognize yourself, your clients, and others with whom you have negotiated.

The Bottom-Liner

Bottom-liners are people who don't like to negotiate or don't feel they have to do so. They are quick to get to the bottom line and put their best offer on the table. Bottom-liners often lack patience, an important quality of a skilled negotiator. A bottom-line strategy works best when one party is in a much stronger bargaining position than the other. For example, if a buyer knows a seller may soon lose his house to foreclosure the buyer can make a "take it or leave it" offer. If the offer is marginally acceptable the seller is often in too weak a position to refuse.

A bottom-line strategy usually doesn't work well when the parties have equal bargaining power. In such situations the bottom-liner can appear controlling and offend the other party with a "take it or leave it" offer. Sometimes a buyer will say that this is the best offer (when it's really not) as a means of testing where the seller is in the negotiation. Some sellers will give in to the buyer's demand out of fear of losing a good prospect. However, this is a dangerous strategy if the buyer really wants the property. If the seller does not give in, the buyer has little choice but to increase the offer. This makes the buyer appear like she is playing games. Many sellers will react negatively to such game playing, and will either play games of their own or punish the buyer by being less willing to compromise on price. Bottom-liners stuck in this position often end up paying more for property than they would have had they not drawn an arbitrary line in the sand.

When the parties are in more equal negotiating positions the best response to a bottom-liner is to keep negotiating and seek further concessions. In such situations bottom-liners are often forced to compromise from their bottom-line positions and end up paying more or taking less.

The "I Lack Authority" Approach

With this negotiating technique a party negotiates on behalf of another but then claims to lack authority to consummate the tentative deal. After negotiations have begun one agent then seeks further concessions due to "unexpected" demands of the principal.

Spouses (particularly where one spouse regularly travels) sometimes use this negotiating technique quite effectively. One spouse will get the negotiations to a certain point only to then claim that the final decision maker in the transaction is the other spouse who must approve an agreement that has been reached in principal.

When only one-half of a couple is involved in the actual negotiations it's a good idea to clarify that they have the authority to act and that the other person is aware of the negotiations. If the person negotiating lacks authority to act the best response is to limit negotiations, or to be equally non-committal until the person with authority is present and participating fully in the negotiations.

Look for clues as to whether this is truly a strategy being employed or a simple and unintended error. Sometimes one member of a couple will exceed the authority given to them by their partner. When this occurs the party who exceeded the authority will call and apologetically explain what happened. She will be very embarrassed and looking to appease the other side in the negotiations. Sometimes a minor concession will be all it takes to get everyone together.

The Good Guy/Bad Guy Routine

The good guy/bad guy routine is frequently used in negotiations to buy and sell homes. There are a couple of variations. The first is where buyers or sellers are a couple. One is very nice and the other one pretends to be (or actually is) not very nice. The second is where the buyer or seller is the bad guy and the real estate agent representing them is the good guy. While in some instances the parties are merely acting out their respective roles, usually the roles come quite naturally.

In basic good guy/bad guy routine, the bad guy makes an appearance during the negotiation and, of course, acts badly. After giving the bad impression the bad guy retreats from the scene and the good guy negotiates the deal. The good guy makes frequent references to the bad guy's unreasonableness as the basis for obtaining concessions in the negotiations. The theory of this approach is that the party on the other side of the negotiation will so dislike the "bad guy" that she will gravitate toward the good guy and try to strike a deal with her.

The following statement by the buyer to her agent or to the listing agent is typical of what the good guy in the relationship might say:

> *"You know, as you saw when we visited the property, my husband can be strong-willed. He owns his own company and is used to making snap decisions. I really like the house, but he thinks the price is too high because of the needed repairs. Frankly, I'm trying to figure out a way to buy this house. I'm just going to have to get the seller to either agree to reduce the price or make more repairs."*

The wife is asking her agent to participate in a little "conspiracy" to help her buy the house. The concessions are being sought to make her husband happy (not because they are necessarily rational or fair). This "good guy" wife is always sympathetic toward and understanding of the other party's position. She will either take the other side's position or act like she is just in the middle trying to get the deal done. As a mediator, the good guy seeks concessions (even unreasonable ones) in a non-offensive way under the guise of merely trying to please her unreasonable partner.

Real estate agents can effectively play this same game by describing their client or clients in bad-guy terms. This technique works best when a party is seeking major financial concessions from the other (such as a large reduction in the sale price) but wants to do so in an inoffensive way. Where the seller has no need or incentive to make such a concession the strategy rarely works. This strategy can backfire when sellers have lived in a home for a long time, treat it as a prized possession, and want it to only go to nice people who will enjoy it as much as they have. (At this point you will be very glad you asked the seller's agent all those questions we suggested in Rule No. 3. If you are thus prepared you will likely have clues as to when this strategy may backfire.)

The counter-strategy to a good guy/bad guy routine is to try to take advantage of the good guy's agreeable nature and lock her into agreeing with your basic position. You can then respond with a divide-and-conquer strategy by trying to isolate the unreasonable party. A sample line might be, "I'm sorry we can't come to terms, particularly since you and I agree on what's fair. I hope you can persuade your client [or partner] to come around."

The "Now You've Made Me Mad" Approach

As we mentioned in the previous chapter, feigning anger or righteous indignation is a tactic often used by one party to extract concessions from the other.

Imagine calling a listing agent to report that the seller's counteroffer has been rejected by the buyer. The buyer's agent explains the counteroffer that will be sent. The listing agent erupts and says, "I can't believe your buyer didn't accept the offer. It was an incredible offer and far less than the property is worth. I told the seller she shouldn't have made such a generous offer and now you're telling me it has been rejected by the buyer? Are you kidding me? Don't make any counteroffer until you and your client have thought long and hard about it."

Human nature is such that we often try to placate people who are angry with us. The "now you've made me mad" approach essentially uses anger and intimidation to try to achieve goals.

The best response is to keep your cool, do not respond defensively, and do not take it personally. While some parties genuinely enjoy being hostile and aggressive, it must be remembered that the use of this technique is just a ploy designed to achieve a specific end. There are several ways to respond to this type of tactic.

The smartest is to ignore it and act like you are having the most pleasant conversation in the world with the angry party. Without question, this takes practice.

In response to the angry listing agent mentioned earlier you might say, "Well, I really think your client is going to like this latest counteroffer. I'll send it over now for you to present to your client." Taking the bait and starting to argue over the merits of the seller's original counteroffer (which your client has already rejected) is almost never productive; your ability to negotiate will be compromised.

If the listing agent continues to persist in an overly hostile manner say in a pleasant but firm manner, "We obviously disagree on the price at which the property should sell. While I've heard and understand your position, nevertheless, this is the offer my client has decided to make. Therefore, I will be sending it over to you shortly and direct you to present it to your client immediately for consideration."

The other approach is to say to the listing agent, "It's obvious you are upset. Nevertheless, we both have our respective jobs to do. This is a simple business transaction. The seller can accept or reject the offer. I am going to send the contract over to you and I know you will timely present it as you are required to do."

If you are the one taking this approach you should consider carefully when to employ it as a tactic. If your too-agreeable buyer needs you to be the "bad guy" to try and win some concessions, be sure you let your client know that this is the approach you plan to take and obtain their agreement first. This flies in the face of the more general "be friendly" rule we began with and should be used sparingly.

The Nibbler

The nibbler is someone who either intentionally or unintentionally has difficulty making a decision regarding the purchase or sale of real estate, and usually everything else as well. It's the buyer who visits a property a dozen times yet can't quite get to the point of making an offer. While some might think being a nibbler is not a negotiating style at all, hanging around the scene as a prospective buyer (particularly if the seller doesn't have other hot prospects) definitely wins concessions (often unsolicited) from the seller or listing agent.

One of the authors had an experience as a nibbler on a recent business trip to Cozumel. He was looking for a gift to bring back to his family and couldn't decide whether a particular gift was appropriate. Although the author normally makes decisions quickly, in this instance he waited in the store thinking about whether he wanted the gift or not. The store was not particularly crowded and the store clerk knew the author was having a hard time making a decision. The author asked the clerk a lot of questions about the gift, and the clerk did the best he could to answer them.

After a while the sales clerk indicated that if the author bought the gift he would give him a significant discount. As the author continued to vacillate the clerk reduced the price of the gift a second, and eventually a third and fourth time – all without the author having made a single offer!

While we would never expect this to occur in a real estate transaction, this approach is most effective with a house that has been on the market a while without any serious prospects. A good real estate agent will not allow a buyer to linger without trying to learn the obstacles to purchasing the property and if they can be overcome.

Nibblers also gain an advantage through the investment of time they make in a property. It is to the nibbler's advantage if the listing agent spends a lot of time trying to put together a deal. To the extent the listing agent feels psychologically invested in the nibbler, the greater the likelihood the agent will recommend or make the needed concessions to put the deal to bed.

If you are on the other side of a transaction from the nibbler-buyer, the best way to get a commitment is to raise the specter of another interested buyer. The nibblers' strongest card is a lack of interest in the property by other buyers. If another buyer enters the scene many nibblers will commit if they have a good deal and don't want to lose the property.

The Expert

The expert uses her knowledge (real or perceived) as a tool to convince the other party to the negotiation of the correctness of her position. The expert is a know-it-all. She is quick to tell you the "facts" as she sees them and to refer to her many years of experience to support her expert position. Most real experts have little need to tell you of their expertise and doing so is usually off-putting to the other party.

With respect to the value of a property the expert might say something like, "Look, I've been buying and selling real estate for thirty years. I know what properties sell for and I can tell you when property is overpriced. This property will sell in the $375,000 – $395,000 price range. It won't sell for the $425,000 your seller says is his bottom line. We might be able to get a deal done if the seller will only get a little more realistic about her price." A less-experienced "expert" might talk about her exhaustive research of prices other homes sold for in the neighborhood to argue for a lower valuation on the property.

How does one deal with such an expert? Normally the best approach is to listen to what the "expert" has to say without debating its validity. Sometimes an expert will truly be an expert and something can be learned from what she has to say. Debating the facts is normally counterproductive and rarely leads to either party changing her views. It also misses a basic point of real estate negotiation; the seller is free to offer her property for sale at whatever price the seller wishes, regardless of whether there are "facts" to support her position.

A side-stepping strategy which doesn't focus on the facts is often the best way to deal with an expert. The following response might be appropriate: "Well, the price might be high or the price might be right on the money. Fortunately we only need to find one buyer willing to buy the property at this price, and I happen to think that buyer is out there. If your buyer doesn't want to pay this price my client will understand. If you are right and it turns out the price is high, the market will tell us that and the price will be adjusted."

The Desperate Seller

As strange as it may seem, portraying yourself as desperate can be an effective negotiation strategy in certain limited circumstances in which the seller must sell her property. Rather than hiding the fact of her desperation, the seller embraces this status and tries to make lemonade out of lemons by maximizing the seller's return on the property to be liquidated. The success of this approach often depends on the lack of knowledge of the buyer as to the true value of the property and her strong desire to get a bargain. Often this can cloud the buyer's judgment and cause the buyer to pay more for a property than she might have had this strategy not been employed.

Auctioneers often use this strategy with great success in auctioning off lots, condominium units, and other types of real property. They advertise the dream of a great deal to lure large numbers of buyers to the auction to bid on the property being sold. While buyers will usually pay less than the original sale price of the property, we have routinely seen buyers pay significantly more for property being auctioned than the price at which they could have purchased the property immediately prior to the auction.

This same strategy is often used by other sellers as well. A review of the classifieds will often reveal numerous advertisements with phrases like "desperate seller - bring us an offer," "property selling for $100,000 below appraised value," "buy it before the bank forecloses," or "highly motivated seller." Why advertise a distress sale? The answer is the same one which (in less regulated times) caused some oriental rug dealers to have "going out of business" sales that lasted years or decades at a time: there is a breed of buyer who will impulsively pursue a bargain even on things about which they know little. Sellers often demand quick action from the buyers because of the seller's "desperate" situation. Whether the time urgency is the result of real desperation on the part of the seller or to give the buyer less time to evaluate the true merits of the deal will depend on the sophistication and "hucksterism" of the seller. Knowing as P. T. Barnum once said that "a sucker is born every minute," how does a buyer protect herself in these situations?

The answer is twofold. First, never negotiate to buy anything if its true value is unknown. (See Chapter 5 for an in-depth discussion of this point.) This is because the property selling for $100,000 below the appraised value may truly be a bargain, or the appraisal may have been flat wrong. The second word of advice is to go slow with deals that the other party claims must be consummated immediately.

As your experience level increases you may identify other approaches as well, or see variations on the ones we've listed. Know your own personality and tendencies toward a particular style. Be on the lookout so your own style does not hinder your progress in a negotiation.

Mastering the thirty rules we've covered in the past few chapters, and learning to recognize and apply as necessary the various negotiating postures we've described, will make your negotiations more successful. But just mastering a set of "rules" or "techniques" is not enough in the complex game of real estate negotiating. There is another, more inward, arena that needs to be mastered. Our next chapter will take you on a tour of that arena and give you some tips on how to use it to your greatest advantage.

Chapter 13

THE INNER GAME OF NEGOTIATING

Conscious Detachment

In addition to the techniques and approaches we have outlined in our previous chapters, there is another, inner arena we need to master: our minds. There are two distinct parts of this inner arena that we will focus on: self-awareness and other-awareness. Together they create mindset we refer to as "consciously detached," and it is crucial to your success as a negotiator. The two factors of this mindset are so powerful their absence can sabotage the outward negotiating game (no matter how expert are your techniques), and their active participation can propel your negotiating game through the roof (even with less than perfect technique). Learn the techniques and tools by all means, but do not go into any negotiation until you've sharpened your inner game!

This idea of the inner game is not new. In 1974 Timothy Gallwey wrote a phenomenal book titled The Inner Game of Tennis. It was not just another book about the right way to hold a tennis racket, or the best way to use your footwork to your advantage, or how to develop a killer serve. It was about the game that goes on between your two ears. The inner game. He explains that the biggest complaint sports players typically have with their own game is not a problem of technique. "It's not that I don't know what to do, it's that I don't do what I know!" (Gallwey, The Inner Game of Tennis, 1974.)

That truth applies to real estate negotiation as well. At least some of the techniques in this book are things you already know and perhaps even do, but for some reason your negotiating game does-n't quite come together as you would like. Perhaps your focus is off, or you don't stay as calm as you would like, or a certain type of personality on the other side always pushes your hot buttons. Learning to be consciously detached is the key.

To explain what we mean by being consciously detached it will help to remind you of an old poem. Do you remember the story about the blind men and the elephant? To the blind man who touched the tail, the elephant was like a rope; to the one who touched the leg, the elephant was like a tree; to the one who touched the tusk, the elephant was like a spear; and to the one who touched the trunk, the elephant was like a snake. None of them was correct because none of them had all the information needed. When you do not have all the information your conclu-sions will most likely be wrong.

The same is true in negotiations. In order to have a complete pic-ture of the situation you need to draw on information from sev-eral sources. You will of course rely on your knowledge of the market, of the subject property, of your client's goals and of your own role as a negotiator. You also need to have a heightened awareness of the words, actions and body language of the parties with whom you are negotiating. Put yourselves in their shoes for awhile and walk around in them. As you are meeting or speaking with, or listening to, the other party, repeatedly ask yourself ques-tions like the following:
• Are the actions of the other party different from her words or deeds?
• Has the other party or their agent let slip any remark which would indicate a different position from the one they are espousing?

- Does the position of the other party make sense based on what I know about her?
- Are there any details in their unspoken message which might lead me to a different conclusion about the motivations, flexibility and goals of the other party?

This is what we mean by being consciously detached. A great negotiator needs to consciously choose to detach from (while still observing) her own emotional reactions, so that she can observe, focus and concentrate on the behavior of the others in the room. Think of conscious detachment as the coin, with self-awareness being one side of the coin, and other-awareness being the flip side. One side deals with being aware of (and not being controlled by) your personal reactions or feelings; the other side deals with trying to understand what is really going on with the other people in the process. Put the two together and you will have a much more complete picture of an entire negotiation.

As we discussed at the beginning of this book, great negotiators know that emotions are a factor in a negotiation but they do not let their own emotions become one of those factors. They do not let their own emotions interfere with their ability to observe, think clearly, strategize, and negotiate for their clients. They use self-awareness (monitoring their own emotional responses and personality weaknesses) to prevent emotion from derailing the negotiation. When they are self-aware, they are free to notice and interpret clues as to what's really going on with the others in the room (other-awareness). They learn to read between the lines and develop an intuition that others lack. (See Chapter 12 on negotiating styles.)

The reason this is so important in a negotiation is that unlike most other activities, people in a negotiation are often trying to hide their true feelings to get the best deal they can. For example, a desperate seller may act like she is "cool as a cucumber" and doesn't need to sell the property in hopes of not having to make significant price concessions. The only problem with this is that most of us are amateurs when it comes to hiding our true feelings. Consciously detached observers can often spot the little signals or inconsistencies which give them a truer picture of the situation. While this technique will not make you a mind-reader, it can give you the information you need to obtain a more complete picture of the elephant. Let's look in greater detail at the self-awareness side of the conscious detachment coin.

Self-Awareness

The self-awareness that we refer to consists of monitoring your emotional responses during a negotiation and using them to your best advantage, rather than allowing them to control what you do. There are at least four reasons why monitoring your emotions (and being in control of them) is so crucial to the negotiation process:

(1) Emotions can reduce a person's ability to observe what is going on around them. You may miss subtle clues that indicate a sea change in the position or approach of the other side;

(2) Emotions can cause a person to say things she later regrets. Anger and frustration can cause hasty, snap decisions – or a too-snappy response that may turn the negotiation in a direction that was not intended;

(3) Emotions can affect the ability of the negotiator to be fully observant of all the data they need to be absorbing during the process. If you are busy thinking about what a "jerk" the other agent is being, you may also fail to notice signs that their own client had the same reaction. That bit of information could be helpful; and

(4) Even if no data is missed, strong emotion can affect a negotiator's ability to process that data accurately.

This emotion-monitoring process is difficult for some to develop and may require practice. Fortunately, it is a skill that you can practice almost anywhere at anytime. Focus on what raises your blood pressure or pushes your buttons in a real estate negotiation. Usually it is a remark made by another agent or that agent's client that impugns your character, challenges your expertise, or is just plain hateful, that prompts you to react in kind. Anticipate and accept that these types of situations will occur in a negotiation. The question then is how you will react to them. We recommend that you think of these situations as if they were a game. Lose your cool, and you lose the game. Keep your cool and you win the game. Look at situations when the party with whom you are negotiating loses their cool as a great opportunity to observe what's really going on inside their head. Your ability to gain insights from these situations will be enhanced if you are emotionally level yourself.

Try practicing this monitoring process when you're discussing something with your teenager, or even with your ex-spouse or someone you've always disliked. After a few practice runs, try it during your next meeting with a prospective client or while showing properties. Little by little your ability to keep your cool will improve and you will become an expert in this monitoring process.

Remember that some parties will intentionally bait you in a negotiation as a way to see what they can learn about you.

We suggest that you spend some time thinking about past negotiations and the incidents where you felt some strong emotional response come up. What type of situations cause that in you? Take note of these situations and perhaps even make a list of them. Then when you are preparing for a negotiation, go over your list. Try to anticipate which of these situations you may see again based on what you have learned about your client, and the agent and principal on the other side. If the situation does not surprise you when it comes up, you are much more likely to be able to handle it well. If a new situation gets you worked up, put it on the list and repeat the process.

Recognizing the types of situations where strong emotion may be triggered in you can be very helpful, but by itself is not enough. You also need to understand how those situations trigger a response in you. Spend some time thinking about your overall personality style and how that can hinder you in a negotiation.

Some people are outgoing and friendly; some are more introverted-thinking types. You may be serious and solemn, or warm and gregarious. You may be naturally logical and methodical, or you may prefer to "trust your gut" as you move through a negotiation. We each bring our individual style of dealing with the world with us into any negotiation, as do our counterparts and our clients. Keeping your emotions in check does not mean trying to become someone you are not. We are suggesting only that you recognize how your personal style may affect a negotiation, and keep the emotional component in check. Use your personal style to your advantage, but do not let your counterpart use your style to their advantage! Let's look at a few examples of what we mean.

The People Person. Many real estate agents are good at what they do in part because they are "people persons," able to easily meet and connect with others, and capable of "reading" where other people are in dealing with life or with the situation before them.

What are the benefits and drawbacks of these traits in a negotiation? The ability to connect is very useful in obtaining clients, but it is not as necessary in a negotiation. You are not there to win friends – but to influence people. It is your ability to "read" the other participants in a negotiation that can give you quite an advantage.

If this is your personality style, use these traits for all they're worth! Use your ability to connect easily with people to help maintain the smooth flow of friendly conversation, all the while observing the reactions of your counterpart as the negotiation proceeds. Is she confident with her position, or does she exhibit signs of some doubt? Are her facts clearly in order, or is there some way she is misconstruing (or misrepresenting) the facts to gain an advantage? Perhaps she is over confident and not seeing the gaping hole in the arguments she is using to further her position. Use your ability to draw people out to get your counterpart to reveal more than she may intend.

Do not, however, let your counterpart use these traits against you. How could that happen? Easy - if you get into a negotiation and find that you are more focused on connecting than you are on observing. Or perhaps your ability to connect with others is accompanied by a strong desire to please people (as is often the case). Be careful. Before you enter a negotiation, focus. Remember your purpose in the negotiation. If you focus on "reading the room" instead of befriending it, you'll be fine.

The Cool Cucumber. Let's say you are the agent who is by nature cool as a cucumber, analytical, and always thinking. You are the professional for whom focusing on the facts comes naturally. Once clients understand the depth of your expertise, they willingly entrust their search for a home (or the sale of their home) to you. Now you come to the negotiation stage. What are the benefits of this personality style? It is easy for you not to let your emotions interfere with your ability to observe, think clearly, strategize, and negotiate for your clients. Emotions do not enter into your equation. Beware, however, of your potential weakness. You may have difficulty recognizing the emotions of your clients and other parties during the negotiation process. By leaving the emotions of the other participants out of your equation, you may miss out on some tactical advantage and your great strength can become your great weakness. You need to pay attention to the emotional cues of your counterpart, and of your clients, as the negotiation proceeds.

While you are watching the other parties' emotions for clues, and watching your own for hints that your counterpart's strategy may be getting to you, do not let emotion control your actions or words. Do not let your emotions interfere with your ability to negotiate for your clients. As we have said, this is a hard skill to develop.

Other-Awareness

When you have learned to be more in control of your emotions, you are more free to become other-aware. The consciously detached negotiator assumes that very few of the interactions constituting the negotiation are random or without some specific meaning or design. If a person is acting in a particular way or saying a specific thing, the assumption is that there is some significance that action or word has to the negotiation. Of course as Phaedrus once said, "Things are not always as they seem." Becoming "other-aware" requires an ongoing internal dialogue to help identify the method to the madness of someone else's words or behavior.

As you participate in the discussion let the observing part of you stand back a bit and listen. The observer analyzes every word, action, or emotion of the other participant.

A great negotiator must be functioning on many levels at the same time. The adrenaline is pumping. You are on the playing field, so to speak, and it's showtime. Yet you also must be the coach sitting on the sidelines watching carefully, alert to changes in your team's field position that may require tactical adjustments. You must be consciously detached from the action in which you participate. You are not only taking in the details of your counterpart's stated position, but also observing her tone, body language, and the way her offer or counteroffer is packaged. You are monitoring your client's emotional temperature, tone and body language. And you are keeping a handle on your own emotions so they don't surprise you and trip you up as you proceed.

There may be occasions when an agent chooses to display some feigned emotion in a negotiation. For example, using the "now you've made me mad" approach to try to extract some concessions from the other side. But this is different from letting your emotions control you. It is an intentional, thought-out approach that results from cool judgment, rather than an emotional reaction that clouds your judgment. Learn the difference well and learn to recognize it in others.

The concentration it takes to intentionally observe and constantly ask yourself questions about the other party's motivations, while seemingly engaging in a normal conversation with the other party, is immense. With practice, negotiators can master the skills of being consciously-detached provided they have all of their wits about them. Being emotional makes it almost impossible to play this key role. When the urge to respond emotionally arises learn to count to ten, bite your lip, or effect a strategic withdrawal and live to negotiate another day.

Chapter 14

THERE'S A FLAG ON THE PLAY
Avoiding Legal Trouble

The techniques described in this book encourage real estate negotiators to take an active role in negotiating on behalf of their clients. With this increased role comes the possibility of greater potential legal liability. It is, therefore, critical that agent negotiators take steps to minimize their legal risks.

Real estate agents who are truly serious about becoming all-star real estate negotiators must have a solid grasp of the laws governing their activities. In most cases this requires training that goes far beyond that required to obtain a real estate license. Most pre-licensure courses teach the minimum needed to pass the real estate examination. Unfortunately, taking and passing a written licensure test is simply not going to prepare most people for the legal issues they will face being a real estate agent.

The laws governing real estate agents vary considerably from state to state. For example, in some states real estate agents are permitted to draft fairly extensive special stipulations, significantly modifying their form contracts. In others this is considered the unlicensed, and illegal, practice of law. In some jurisdictions agents and sellers are required to use mandatory disclosure forms. In others the rule is caveat emptor, or buyer beware.

A detailed state-by-state analysis of real estate law is beyond the scope of this book. You should, however, obtain a copy of your state's laws regulating real estate brokerage and agency and a copy of the rules and regulations of all real estate commission or similar governing bodies to which you are subject. Study and learn these laws and regulations until you have a good, thorough, working knowledge of them. If they are complicated or don't make sense to you, ask someone more experienced to walk you through them, take continuing education courses, or hire a knowledgeable real estate brokerage attorney to tutor you.

Finally, you should study and understand the National Association of REALTORS® Code of Ethics, and know like the back of your hand the terms and inner workings of any form contracts used in your jurisdiction. While this will take time and may involve some expense, it is your real estate license we are talking about. You worked hard to obtain it; make sure you work hard to protect and keep it.

The following general guidelines will help you steer clear of many legal hurdles and avoid crossing the line on tough ethical dilemmas. Many of these guidelines have been discussed in earlier chapters. Here we will address how following them can minimize the likelihood of having any legal claim filed against you. However, these are only general guidelines. This is not intended to be legal advice. You should follow your state's laws whenever they conflict with what follows.

Don't Make Guaranties or Promises You Can't Keep.

Promote yourself as a skilled negotiator. Let prospective clients know that your skills are valuable and worth the cost. However, be sure you know your limitations. It may be okay to promise you will take some action, but do not guarantee the results. If, for example, you convince a client to use you as a full-service agent by guaranteeing they "will save $10,000" you need to be able to deliver on your promise. Otherwise you will have an unhappy client more likely to assert a claim against you.

By contrast, it is easier to back up a promise that you will "do everything you can to save the client $10,000" or that you will "work hard" to help the client achieve her stated goals. Of course the best practice is to not to make any guarantees at all. If you must make guarantees, keep them non-specific and focus on how you will do something as opposed to the result you will obtain. And before making any guarantee, particularly if it is included in any advertisement, you need to be sure you are not inadvertently violating any applicable fair trade practices act or other law in your state.

Keep Your Client Informed.

It is easy to say that you need to keep your client informed, but this can be far more difficult to do in practice. We live in a busy world and it's easy to get distracted. It is critical, however, that you take the time to keep your client informed of every significant event related to your representation.

For example, your client should receive a copy of each and every document that comes into your hands relative to their transaction. With the exception of your personal notes, their file should contain everything yours does. We suggest you even make up a file folder for your client at the beginning of your representation. Explain your plan to keep them informed, and that they will be receiving a copy of everything from you. That file is to help them keep track of the entire process. Similarly, you should inform your client of every pertinent meeting or conversation you have with anyone concerning their transaction. Be sure you keep notes in your own file of the date and time of any such meetings or conversations, as well as the date and time you relayed the information to your client.

Finally, never end a conversation or meeting with your client without: (a) confirming that the client understands what you have just told her, (b) confirming her understanding of what will happen next, and (c) asking if she has any questions.

Don't Delay Giving Bad News.

It is human nature to dread delivering bad news. It also goes against the grain of most real estate agents who work hard to promote the sale. Sometimes agents convince themselves that it's okay to wait a while before telling their client something unpleasant on the hope that the passage of time will cause the problem to "go away" or correct itself.

We have seen this happen, for instance, when the buyer's earnest money check bounced. The agent, believing the buyer's story that he simply did not transfer funds into the account quickly enough, deposited the check again without notifying the seller. Meanwhile the seller, who was oblivious to the potentially failing contract, signed a contract to purchase another property. When the buyer's funds were never made good the agent was eventually forced to disclose what occurred. The seller was furious, and rightfully so. Had she known there was a problem with the buyer she might not have contracted to purchase the other house. We are aware of several instances when this unfortunate scenario resulted in the unhappy agent purchasing the seller's property to avoid being sued.

Put It in Writing.

If everyone always told the truth and always did what is right, lawyers would need to find something else to do. People do not always do what they should and frequently their recollection of what was said or disclosed changes over time ... or when it suits their needs (like when they are on the witness stand). Failure to put facts in writing can later pit agent against client. The judge or jury must decide whom to believe.

The best way to avoid this situation is to put important items in writing. While people may still differ on what they remember, it is much more difficult to refute what is in someone's notes that were made at the time of the conversation. The obvious question is "how do I decide what is sufficiently important to commit to writing?" There are a few ways to handle this. For some, it simply makes sense to keep notes of everything that happens. For others, just making notes of the date and time a conversation took place and of the final outcome of the discussion is sufficient. Perhaps the best litmus test is this: when you find yourself thinking "I wonder if this is something I should put in writing?" then you probably should.

When in Doubt, Disclose.

Subject to your state's disclosure rules, the best practice is to err on the side of disclosure. Very few claims can be maintained on the basis that the agent disclosed too much about a property. On the other hand, many claims can be brought on the basis that the agent either neglected to make a disclosure or, worse, intentionally failed to do so. The most common claims we see against real estate agents are for negligence and fraud related to the failure of an agent to make a disclosure.

Keep Your Eye on the Clients' Goal.

Remember that it is your clients' goals you are trying to achieve, not your own. Once you have gotten the result your client wants,

stop. Do not try to impress your client by attempting to negotiate for an even better deal without first getting their consent.
Your well-intentioned efforts just might end up causing your
client to lose the deal. If that happens, no amount of back-ped-
aling is going to save you.

Know Your Limits.

You are a real estate agent and a negotiator. Remember that you
are not a lawyer, home inspector, structural engineer, appraiser,
accountant, etc., unless you actually are. Do not be afraid to let
your client know when they need services that you are not capable of providing, or for which you are not licensed.

Protect Your Credibility.

Some techniques discussed in this book involve deflecting questions that you do not want to answer for fear of hurting your
client's bargaining position. Others discuss ways to pick up clues
about the buyer or seller that might help your clients. There is,
however, a definite and important distinction between giving a
vague response and telling a lie. Likewise, there is a difference
between looking around the visible part of a home for information about the seller and rummaging through their trash can.

Being an aggressive and creative negotiator is great. However,
keep your credibility and reputation in mind. When faced with
a situation in which you think it would be helpful to your client
if you gave a vague answer, first consider what the consequences
would be if the other side learned exactly what you are doing. For
example, the buyer's agent asks if the sellers are getting a divorce.
Instead of saying something non-responsive like "with relationships these days, who knows?" you say, "Absolutely not." The

buyer then sees a notice of the filing of a divorce action in the newspaper. Well, you have just lost credibility. You got caught in a lie. In addition to violating the National Association of REALTORS® Code of Ethics, your effectiveness as a negotiator in this transaction has been reduced to nil.

The Voice in Your Head May Actually Be Telling You Something.

When we interview real estate agents who have been sued they often tell us, "You know, I just knew this deal was going to be a problem." Sometimes they can't articulate what it is that caused them to be wary, but they say "I should have listened to that voice in my head that was trying to tell me something." Trust your instincts. If you sense a problem coming, try to head it off by documenting everything and being ultra-communicative with your clients.

At other times rather than a whispered voice you may sense more of a wildly waving red flag. Maybe the seller had three prior agents all of whom she describes as "incompetent." Perhaps the buyer refuses to have the house inspected. Any number of things can be cause for alarm. The more red flags that are waving, the more diligent and careful you need to be.

Not All Clients Are Worth Having.

Remember that not all clients are worth having. Some will demand that you do something illegal, such as not disclose a defect of which you might be aware. Others will want you to do something that, while not necessarily illegal, does not allow you to sleep at night. These are the times when it is best to walk away from the transaction. Tell your client that you are sorry, but you cannot continue to work for them. Terminate the relationship. A person who asks you to break the law or who pressures you to take a posture you are not comfortable with is also a person who does not respect you. They are very likely to be the first to turn on you the moment something goes wrong or if they do not get a result they like. Run, do not walk, to the nearest exit.

Don't Hesitate to Consult an Expert Early.

Finally, if you have a question of a legal or ethical nature, consult an appropriate expert before your question becomes a problem. You can save yourself thousands of dollars (not to mention many nights' sleep) by spending a little money and time consulting an attorney up front before your molehill becomes a full-blown mountain. I guarantee that a consultation fee will be money well-spent, and will be a fraction of the cost to defend a lawsuit or ethics complaint.

Chapter 15

POST-GAME WRAP-UP

After a professional sporting event has ended there are the usual post-game commentaries that follow. After a negotiation has been completed, hopefully resulting in a deal with good results for you and your client, it is also a good idea to do some wrapping-up of the process. While we do not suggest spending hours with your client re-hashing every phase of a negotiation, there are some things that definitely should be covered. Put the negotiation and its results in the spotlight a bit, and review with your client what has been accomplished – and what remains to be done.

What Has Been Accomplished

When you have clearly achieved a good result it is easy to identify and review what has been accomplished. You should review the clients' stated goals with them and verify their agreement that the goals have been met. This may mean discussing the way that particular time constraints were successfully dealt with, or discussing with buyer clients how the specific features of the property they are purchasing meet their needs, or discussing with selling clients the great price you were able to negotiate for them.

The purpose here is to confirm your clients' positive experience. It's like the pat on the back to a teammate when you've just won the game. As we have discussed, the most difficult part of the negotiation may have been dealing with the last few issues. You want your clients to have a sense of accomplishment as a result of the process rather than simply feeling exhausted or "glad that's over with."

If a negotiation has not resulted in a satisfactory deal, the agent may need to draw on both tact and some rose-colored glasses to highlight what has been accomplished. Are your buyer clients now clearer about their goals? Are they better educated about the process and therefore prepared for a more effective negotiation on another property? Have mortgage rates or the market become more favorable to buyers during the negotiation process? Cast the negotiation in the best light possible, encourage your clients that the perfect property for them may be literally just around the corner, and affirm your commitment to help them locate and acquire it. Schedule your next appointment with them to fine-tune their goals and to map out your strategy for finding that perfect property.

If you represented the sellers and a negotiation did not result in a sale you would take a similar approach. Are the sellers now clearer about the process? More realistic as to the true value of their property? Perhaps the market has become more favorable to sellers during the negotiation, or some future neighborhood change has become known that increases the marketability of their property. Again, you want to cast the negotiation in the best possible light and confirm your commitment to the sellers that you are still on the same team. Set up your next appointment with them to review any changes to your game plan and begin preparation for the next negotiation.

What Remains to be Done

If no deal is reached in your negotiation the next steps are simple: go back to the beginning and your behind-the-scenes work. Before your next meeting with your clients review what you know (and what you've learned during the recent negotiation) regarding your client's goals, property values, market conditions, as well as how your clients' personalities and tactics affected the negotiation. Consider your own performance, and determine ways you can improve your approach and handling of the next negotiation, including your handling of your clients. (Does the wizard need to remain behind the curtain next time?)

Was your recommendation regarding a listing price reasonable, or is that something that needs to change? If the property has been given significant exposure and yet receives little or no traffic, it has probably been overpriced. If there has been significant traffic yet few (or no) offers, there may be a problem with the property itself, hopefully one that can be corrected with a few coats of paint or some minor landscaping additions. Prepare yourself to candidly discuss these issues with your clients even though it may be uncomfortable to do so.

Then go to work with your clients. Communication is key. Educate them, if necessary, about property values, market conditions, etc. Re-clarify their goals. Be sure you are on the same page with them, update the game plan, and set your strategy.

When a deal has been reached, however, there are many things that must be done in order to successfully close the transaction. Inspections often need to be made. Financing arrangements need to be set in motion. Appraisals or surveys may need to be obtained. While a detailed overview of these issues is beyond the scope of this book, remember that one of your business goals is to develop a good relationship with these clients. You want them to be so well-satisfied with your representation that they become a good source of referral and even repeat business. You want your clients to understand what their responsibilities are under the negotiated deal, and to follow-up with them to ensure timely compliance.

It will benefit no one if you manage to negotiate a terrific deal only to have it fall apart for lack of timely follow-through.

Congratulations! You've learned how to become a master at understanding the value of a property and its market context. You've practiced ways to identify and strengthen your best arguments in a negotiation, how to ask the right questions, and to anticipate those you will be asked. You are familiar with the tools you will need and the techniques that will help you utilize them. You know the rules, and you're ready to hit the field running. You are ready to negotiate with confidence and excellence.

Go forth and successfully multiply your business!

.